This is a tremendously helpful and timely book. The Christian discussing pacifism ought to know something about the various types of pacifism, and here he can learn a great deal.

Some people will be surprised to learn that there are at least twenty-five identifiable types of religious pacifism. Seventeen types are treated in depth in this book, and eight more in a brief manner.

These types are not presented as being mutually exclusive. Indeed, the pacifist reader will be surprised at how many types he finds within himself. And the nonpacifist reader may be surprised that there are so many ways of arguing against war.

The book is generously sprinkled with the kind of new and refreshing insights many readers have come to expect of this author.

Future discussions of pacifism will profit by using the typology of this book. Communication will be improved as varieties of pacifism can be identified by name.

— *John K. Stoner*
   Executive Secretary-Elect
   Peace Section (U.S.)
   Mennonite Central Committee

Christian Peace Shelf Series

This title, *Nevertheless*, is sponsored by the Institute of Mennonite Studies, Elkhart, Indiana, and published by Herald Press, Scottdale, Pennsylvania.

The Christian Peace Shelf is a series of books and pamphlets devoted to the promotion of Christian peace principles and their applications. The editor, appointed by the Mennonite Central Committee Peace Section, and an editorial board from the Brethren in Christ Church, General Conference Mennonite Church, Mennonite Brethren Church, and Mennonite Church, represents the historic concern for peace within these brotherhoods.

NEVERTHELESS

*The Varieties and Shortcomings
of
Religious Pacifism*

John H. Yoder

HERALD PRESS
Scottdale, Pennsylvania
Kitchener, Ontario

Related books by John H. Yoder
The Christian and Capital Punishment (Faith and Life Press)
The Christian Pacifism of Karl Barth (Distributed by Herald Press)
The Christian Witness to the State (Faith and Life Press)
Karl Barth and the Problem of War (Abingdon Press)
The Original Revolution (Herald Press)
The Politics of Jesus (Eerdmans)
Reinhold Niebuhr and Christian Pacifism (Out of Print)

NEVERTHELESS
Copyright © 1971 by Herald Press, Scottdale, Pa. 15683
    Published simultaneously in Canada by Herald Press,
    Kitchener, Ont. N2G 1A7
Library of Congress Catalog Card Number: 75-170197
International Standard Book Number: 0-8361-1661-5
Printed in the United States of America
Second Edition, 1976

Gratefully Dedicated

To the many friends,
some still militant and some triumphant,
whose different styles of pacifist commitment
have judged and enriched my own.

Contents

Preface

One of the constants of serious discussion about the Christian's participation in war is the nagging feeling the observer gets that the parties are talking past each other. This mutual misunderstanding is conditioned partly by simple ignorance, in that some of the major Christian pacifist traditions are small and not theologically articulate in "mainstream" terms. It is also part of each thinker's personal history, as when Karl Barth and Emil Brunner react to the pacifism of Leonhard Ragaz, or Reinhold Niebuhr to that of the Fellowship of Reconciliation, of which he had been a member. Some such failure to mesh with the interlocutor is a normal trait whenever there is any really serious difference. But must the parties be this far apart?

In order to bring some clarity to the many-sided conversation about war which the escalation of armament and the Vietnam hostilities have helped to open in recent decades, there is thus need for a far greater awareness that "pacifism" is not just one specific position, spoken for authoritatively by one thinker, but rather a wide gamut of varying, sometimes even contradictory, views. Rather than plunging ahead to debate "right" or "wrong," we must therefore understand each position seriously for what it says and assumes rather than assuming we grasp it adequately by the label it has been given.[1]

We begin, then, by classifying the various positions to which current labels actually already refer. There is no such thing as a single position called "pacifism," to which one clear definition can be given and which is held by all "pacifists." There is rather a congeries of varied kinds of opposition to war; some of them run parallel but some are very different from one another in accent and sometimes even in substance. They can be grouped together under the same label only by doing violence to one or the other. What we undertake is thus what could be called a "typology," asking how many different types of pacifism there are and how they differ from one another. Or we could call it a "topology," an effort somehow to place the various positions "on the map." We must seek in their relations to each other, some as near neighbors and some as quite distant, to look at each in its own logical right before leaping ahead to an evaluation, rather than assigning to one position or to all of them the flaws we see in one particular variety.

Our concern to perceive each position in its integrity will override even our concern for clarity of analysis. We could have made the job easier for both writer and readers by fitting the "types" of pacifism into the ready-made slots of the ethicists. We could play moralities of means off against moralities of ends; principles versus intuition, conscience versus responsibility, motiva-

tions versus strategy. We have no objection if
the reader sees such classical systematic-ethical
themes showing through, and shall not hesitate
to borrow as shorthand some of these labels
where they fit; but we have chosen not to derive
our outline from such analysis. Such a setting of
alternatives nearly always assumes there is but
one basic question and but two possible answers
to it, letting this polarity dominate all analysis,
whereas to make room for at least three or four
choices would be more fair. Furthermore, it
usually covertly favors one of the two. We here
want each position to spring from its own roots;
we therefore refuse to sanction any one polarity
by pretending that it clarifies and categorizes
more than the others.

It may be possible farther along to classify the
types and note their intrinsic interlockings,
parallels, and overlaps. First, though, we must
discern and report their diversity, discovering the
integrity and the coherence of each. We proceed
more or less in order of decreasing familiarity.[2]

The classification proposed below might not be
recognized by all of the persons described. Many
pacifists are activists and not given to systematic
conceptual analysis. A given individual may com-
bine more than one of these positions within his
own conviction. Labeling different positions and
noticing the differences between them does not
necessarily mean that the borders between them
are airtight. Yet this possibility of overlapping
does not justify placing all these positions "in
one sack" or accusing those who hold one position of the axioms of another.

I.

The Pacifism
of Christian
Cosmopolitanism

*". . . the true and solid peace of
nations consists not in equality of arms,
but in mutual trust alone."*
— *Pope John XXIII*, Pacem in Terris

To understand one way the church may be
concerned about the peace in the world we may
well begin with the picture of a church in a small
town. The Christian church and its pastor in the
village will be concerned not only for the thoughts
and behavior of the members of the congregation
but for the total life of the community. The
church will be concerned for the needs and behavior of nonmembers to the extent to which
they are recognized as neighbors and their action
influences the community atmosphere. The pastor
will not only teach his faithful but will also preach
to the rest of the community that it is both de-

sirable and, in general, possible for neighbors to live together in peace. Should there be disputes between neighbors — and not only if they are church members — the small-town pastor will admonish the participants to get together, to negotiate and be reconciled. He will not necessarily take sides nor seek to be judge between them. He makes his appeal to mature neighborly understanding, without himself judging the merits of any particular conflict.

In this small town there may be a sheriff. He may carry arms and sometimes use them. But most of the time, and in the motivation of most of the citizens, the reason they live together in peace is not that there is a sheriff, but that as intelligent and mature human beings most of them realize that it is most of the time in the interest of most of them to make peaceful relationships — even at the cost of some sacrifice and some accommodation — the foundation of their social relations. The Christians have further reason for peaceful living and the pastor has further reasons for calling for peace, but these reasons generally coincide with the wholesome interest of the whole community.

Now stretch the picture to the worldwide scale. Christians are learning to think globally. This is partly the result of technology, but also partly an effect of the gospel. The church exists, even though feebly, all around the world. She recognizes a responsibility for the whole world as her parish. If then the world is her parish, it is on the world level in the society of nations that she should apply the picture of the community which ought to get along together without violence most

14

of the time. Just as the local society must out-grow being governed by feuds and mafia, just as the border between the United States and Canada is peaceful in the absence of armament rather than because of armament, so on the world level the nations should learn to get along together.

The most striking statements of this position have been those of the popes, beginning with Benedict XV (1914-22), expanding especially in recent decades with *Pacem in Terris*, and cul-minating symbolically with the 1966 speech of Paul VI at the United Nations. The Pope does not assume that all men of good will are Chris-tian, but rather that in the name of God and morality and humanity he can speak even to non-Christians about what constitutes well-being for everyone in his parish. He does not begin with the fundamental question of the morality of war, nor does he attempt to decide in a given conflict which party is in the right; he simply says in a pastoral way that if men are ever going to get along together, squabbling is no help. This type of moral concern is an expression of the pastoral attitude of the church toward all of society includ-ing unbelievers. Or in other words: it is a test and an expression of the genuine catholicity which the church claims. The church confirms, by so speak-ing, that she is not a national or a provincial community. Thus in a broad sense we could call this a "catholic" position. Yet it is not unique to the Roman Church. Numerous Protestants and some secular world federalists would hold the same kind of position. The same stance is also being taken increasingly by the World Council of Churches, and nonreligious purveyors of moral insight can take it as well.

The *axiom* underlying this approach is that our common humanity is both a fact and a moral imperative, and that human community — on every scale from village to globe — both needs and authorizes certain voices to speak for "the peace of the city" as a value in its own right, quite apart from the merits of particular conflicts, and from particular systems of ethical judgment on the morality of killing. Any church or council which sees the world whole will today take that shepherd's stance.

The strength of this approach on the part of the church is symbolized by the United Nations visit, or in the later visit of Soviet President Podgorny to Pope Paul. There is such a thing as moral authority which a person or an institution can carry, which can demand and get a serious hearing from society at large. This is not a constitutional right; it holds true only at certain times and places and on certain subjects. Nevertheless it is a reality to reckon with. Society can be helped in specific cases, quite apart from any change in the religious commitment of individuals, by the ways in which a bearer of moral authority identifies issues and applies the weight of its (or his) prestige.

If we measure this kind of "catholic" pacifism by the standards of Christian moral theology, it has some real shortcomings. Does it not give to society at large the idea that Christianity is basically a set of moral teachings, moral teachings which are sometimes opposed to the true interest and welfare of men and practically im-

16

possible to live up to? Does proclaiming such an understanding of moral demands not give to some men by implication the impression that these demands can be met with human resources alone? Does it not give to others an impression of irrelevance? Can moral exhortation thus speak of what is generally good for society while sidestepping firm commitment on contested matters of morality, such as whether killing itself is ever intrinsically wrong? Just as the earlier expressions of this concern, the medieval institutions of the Peace of God and the Truce of God, legitimized feudal war backhandedly in the course of their efforts to limit it, might not this separation of "pastoral" concern from ethical rigor undercut its own real intent?

Another general weakness is that this kind of moral authority is very easily discredited where it has been called on too often and not heard. Where war is very likely or is already being waged, this kind of admonition cannot stop it. It cannot prevent the explosion of hostilities where men or nations have already ceased to think of one another as belonging to the same society.

Such a "pastoral" concern for all the world can also fail to take sides when the truth does demand a recognition that both parties are not equally to blame.[3]

Nevertheless, even with all of the serious shortcomings, this "catholic" or "pastoral" peace concern is still morally superior to any of the various types of religious provincialism which are the only alternatives to it. Such provincialism in which a church identifies with and thereby absolutizes morally a given nation, renouncing the

17

possibility of standing in judgment over that province or nation because it turns against all the world, is subject to all the same weaknesses just mentioned, but in addition it abandons the world orientation.[4]

Whenever war actually does break out this results in a diminution of the existing communities. In order to pursue the Vietnam War the United States has contributed to the breakdown of NATO; to back up its invasions threatened in Cuba and actual in the Dominican Republic the United States decreased its loyalty to the decision-making power of the Organization of American States. Thus it is not only against a particular enemy people that a war is directed; it also destroys each time a wider fabric of community.[5]

After all, even the most convinced advocate of military violence still applies this "catholic" attitude within his own country. The Pentagon would not approve of having armies along both sides of the Potomac River and along every state line as the only way to keep the peace among the fifty states. Such a renunciation of violence between the several provinces of a nation is taken for granted even by the military. So the real issue is not whether it is possible or wise to renounce violence within a given realm but whether the realm in question must necessarily be the nation or could possibly be a larger segment of the world. The Pentagon agrees that war is wrong between Arizona and California or between the Southern States and New England, or even between the United States and Canada; and by not preparing for it, assures that it will not happen. The only question on which the Pentagon and the pacifist differ is the *size* of the community within which internal warfare is wrong.

What made peace possible, or war impossible, between Pennsylvania and New Jersey, was not that one of them finally won a war against the other. The maintenance of peace by that means tends with time to foster further fragmentation. What made permanent peace possible between two states was their acceptance, on a scale far broader and on a level far deeper than the juridical, of an already given commonality.

But Christians are by definition committed to positing the larger commonality of mankind, rather than the territorial unit, as their homeland. Thus the prerequisites for not needing war are present. Any disorder is a family offense to be dealt with by adjustments within the framework of mutual acceptance, not on the model of a clan conflict or the repression of the outsider.

II.

The Pacifism of the Honest Study of Cases

> *"Some decades ago war may have been an instrument which, although it was brutal, could be used to resolve intolerable international tension; but today, owing to the fact that it cannot be controlled, it has lost even this shred of utility. . . . It has become so colossal that it can no longer exercise any sensible function."*
>
> — *Emil Brunner*, The Divine Imperative

Part of any honestly disciplined approach to ethical decision is what is technically called "casuistry," the application of one's general moral orientation to particular decisions. With regard to this problem of war there is an ancient tradition whose purpose (not necessarily the same as its achievement) has been to do just this, namely to look *case* by *case* at every possible war and to distinguish between those which are purely wrong and those which may be justifiable.

Such a position does not grant that war is always right, which would be to sell out morally to whatever government wants to do. Nor does this position believe that it is possible for the church to call upon the state to help her in her theological concerns with a holy war or crusade. To be honest we can at most say, according to this line of thought, that war might sometimes be justifiable. This then obligates one to study in detail the characteristics of a particular case. One must evaluate the cause for which a war is fought, the authority in whose name it is undertaken, and the methods used.

The *axiom* underlying "just war pacifism" is that every ethical decision must be made concretely. One must not sell out in advance either to the decision made by a government in favor of war or to an absolute principled pacifism adopted prior to the measurement of the exact form of a given war. Moral integrity is a matter of making one's decisions by applying critically and rigorously to given cases the general commitments which one has promised to measure them by. If there is no prior commitment to objective standards, one is not morally accountable. Thus the prior public statement of one's standards, and a commitment to their application, does not sacrifice one's freedom to make decisions in the situation; it is rather the only safeguard that one can remain free, in the face of a given future pressure for decision, to say no if that is the necessary answer.

This is not the place to describe in detail what

21

the traditionally defined standards of the "just war" theory have been nor the style of their application.[6] It is sufficient for our purposes to recognize that if this process of moral evaluation is honest, it must at least sometimes be possible for the conclusion reached, when evaluating a particular war or a particular weapon, to be negative. In that case, a war which a given government is waging or wishes to wage must be rejected *not* on the grounds of general pacifism but because when honestly evaluated it is not an acceptable political undertaking even for someone who does not reject all killing.

The new thing today (i.e., in North America in the late 1960's) is that with regard to Vietnam, or to the prospect of nuclear world war, some persons are honest enough in their application of these standards to come up with negative conclusions. With regard, for instance, to the causes for which war is fought, or the authority in whose name it is fought, some wars can today be seen to be imperialistic or aggressive or to have the effect of perpetuating a tyrannical form of government. With regard to the evaluation of methods, some of the characteristics of modern war which are leading an increasing number of persons to a negative conclusion about its admissibility are the destructiveness and incontrollability of nuclear weapons, guerrilla and counter-guerrilla methods, especially painful weapons like napalm or guava bombs, and types of attack which bring suffering especially to noncombatants.

As it has been said before, there is nothing new about the fundamental principles behind this position. The doctrine of the just war has been the official position of all western Christian bodies since the Crusades, with the exception of a few tiny peace churches and a few solitary prophets. All that is changed is the *nature* of the wars to which the standards are to be applied.

The quotation from Emil Brunner (originally 1932)[7] is one of the earliest statements of this position within mainstream Christianity. Brunner drew from this reasoning, which he called "genuine pacifism" as contrasted to absolutist positions, the justification for a kind of conscientious objection based on *just war criteria*. He has been followed in this by Karl Barth, Paul Ramsey, and more recently by many Roman Catholic and Lutheran thinkers.

This position has numerous logical and theological and practical weaknesses. Although it seeks seriously to measure good and evil in causes and methods, it has no clear yardstick for this; especially not for weighing one good value against another. How much freedom is worth how many civilian lives? What is a military target? What is a legitimate government? The logic and the theology of this position assume that these questions can all be given a neat answer; but in fact none of them can.

A second difficulty is that in many cases, having stated such a doctrine seems to have had the effect of dispensing people from applying it carefully. They think the fact that there exists a doctrine of just war constitutes a justification of war in general, whereas, in fact, it constitutes a *denial* that war can ever be generally justified. The legitimacy of armament, for the potentially

23

justified case of war, is not matched with the creation of institutions or techniques for the control of the use of arms in the other cases. Thus the existence of the doctrine has tended to be taken as a proof when as a matter of fact it should have been meant as a question. So it is that great numbers of Christians in the mainstream denominations assume that the theologians have given them grounds for a good conscience in preparing for and waging war, when this is not at all the case, and feel that the recent groundswell of selective objection is revolutionary, when in fact it is traditional.[8]

From a specifically Christian perspective, a further shortcoming is that the content of the just war conceives of the Christian who is making a decision about war as being in the posture of the righteous policeman. It is assumed that this bearer of just authority has the power to obtain what he wants; it only asks when he may use it all, or how much of it he may use when. Thus the entire structure of the doctrine dodges what the New Testament calls the "cross," the serious possibility that the only fate for truth or righteousness in a given situation might be crucifixion, defeat, powerlessness.

We have been noting the internal weakness of the "just war" position as a kind of logic. Now to look at it from the perspective of the non-pacifist, just war pacifism or "selective pacifism" mixes illegitimately the realms of politics and religion, especially when it is appealed to as a justification for conscientious objector status. The criteria by which the "just war objector"[9] measures are the same as those of political judgment: the legitimacy

24

of a government, of a cause, of the instruments of policy. But then he seems, to those he inconveniences, to be simply glorifying political dissent with a religious sanction, and jeopardizing the health of the community by claiming an absolute moral obligation to refuse to support the political decisions of legitimate government, because of a different view of what constitutes legitimate instruments of policy.

Nevertheless, this position is more honest than any of the alternatives available to those who do not reject all war. It rejects the crusade which blesses war, and the fascism which makes the state an autonomous value subject to no criteria of judgment. Saying yes to war subject to some stated conditions is morally more responsible than saying yes with no limits. Applying the conditions seriously to modern war and actually coming up with a negative answer, is more honest than saying that there are limits but never reaching them.

This theory recognizes a criterion of moral judgment superior to the state. It recognizes that the instruments of the state must be used only for modest and finite values rather than being put in the service of a crusade. In any orderly type of society other than an outspoken dictatorship, the language of the just war theory is one of the most appropriate ways to communicate a Christian peace concern to Christians or to others who claim to be honest politicians. Outside the historic peace churches, the language of the just war theory is a most appropriate vehicle of communication since it is the historic position held at least in theory by all the major Christian bodies. It is possible within this framework to ask questions which lead implicitly beyond the limits of the position itself. "If you say not all wars are right, what are the standards which you have to identify those which are wrong? What preparation have you made to be in a position to disobey the government when it plans a wrong war, comparable to the investment of effort and plans your society has made in being ready to serve in a right one?" [10]

To speak against war by means of the language of the just war theory is *not* to impose the Sermon on the Mount on the world. It uses language and criteria which are of recognized appropriateness in the realm of the state, and therefore cannot be brushed off as irresponsible.

It might further be pointed out that this pacifism of borderline casuistry is very logically the first step which an individual takes along the path to a more consistent pacifism. One must first get accustomed to the idea that one might ever say no, and that one might ever apply critical moral criteria to the claims of the government, before one can even conceive of a more radical moral independence. [11]

After all, those who insist on going on beyond just-war limits with a given war are still just-war casuists about the enemy. They justify their own intervention by condemning the "aggression" of the adversary. After the war is won they condemn through judicial process (Nuremberg, Oradour, Eichmann) those leaders on the losing side who failed to disobey their own government. They create or sustain "governments in exile" claiming legitimacy over against the enemy regime, and they publicize the "atrocities" of the opposing army. All the criteria of just-war logic are implicit in such propaganda. To reject the restraints which just-war thought would impose upon one's own violence is to destroy implicitly the case one makes against the enemy for not having observed those same restraints.

III.

The Pacifism of Absolute Principle

> *"When God prohibits killing, He not only forbids brigandage, which is not allowed even by the public laws, but He warns us not to do even those things which are legal among men. And so it will not be lawful for a just man to serve as a soldier . . . nor to accuse anyone of a capital offense, because it makes no difference whether thou kill with a sword or with a word, since killing itself is forbidden."*
> — *Lactantius of Bithynia (ca. 310)*

If there is a God (rather than "God" being simply a code name to refer to man's own best ideas) . . . ;

And *if* God reveals Himself and His will (rather than simply putting a rubber stamp on men's most sincere decisions) . . . ;

And *if* man is in real need of this revelation if he is to be saved and guided (with ignorance and

28

a warped will both being characteristics of his human state)... ;

Then it is logically inevitable that the revealed will of God will be, at least at some points, different in its form and substance from what man would otherwise have thought on the same subject. There must therefore be a limit set to the applicability of man's own common sense and his right to calculate right and wrong. We must expect that there will be points where the will of God will simply have to be taken on the authority of revelation.

Traditional theology has long seen such "revealed principles" in Scripture. In current thought this mode of understanding the origin and content of ethical observations is out of style, but remains a respectable minority position, having in its favor the logic cited above. The changes of theological style have tried to leave this logic behind, but have never really refuted it.

If there be then such a thing as "absolute principles," whether we think we find these expressed in the text of the Ten Commandments or in some other form, it is very likely that the sanctity of human life will be one of them.[12] Such a position can be held in puritanical and legalistic ways, but it need not be. It can be quite at home within a sectarian understanding of the place of the church in the world, but it need not be limited to that context. It can be the expression of naive assumptions about how God gave the Ten Commandments to Israel, but need not be. This position has found its most categorical expression in recent years on the part of the Austrian Roman Catholic theologian

Johannes Ude.[13] The command "Thou shalt not kill" is according to Ude an absolute, admitting of no exceptions. It is on a quite different level of authority from the various other political practices and prescriptions in the Old Testament which still left a place for violence.

The *axiom* underlying this stance is that man is not capable of auto-salvation; that he must be guided through meaningful general directives received by revelation and bearing authority over him. "Revelation" is the religious label; nontheistic moral man will lean in a similar way on similarly structured generalizations which he accepts as coming to him from "reason" or "human dignity" or "the experience of the race."

It is not a significant shortcoming of this position that it can easily be caricatured by the naive who apply it legalistically, in a self-righteous or self-deceiving way, or by the libertines who reject it because they are unaware of their own irrational commitments to authorities outside themselves. Such weak spots are found in every system; their presence is more a fruit of varying levels of sophistication than of differing ethical postures. They are unavoidable if an ethical posture is to be taken by a whole community, by simple and busy people.

The more serious weaknesses are on the logical level. Even the most categorical command is still communicated in human language and carried by human documents. Whether the documents be the human mind or the Old Testament, the meaning of a verbal command is not unequivocal. The giving and receiving of communication, even if it be in the name of God, is subject to shadings of meaning which the habit of thinking of a limited number of absolute principles fails to respect. This is well exemplified by the very case of the Ten Commandments, where the strictest translation would probably read not, "Thou shalt not kill" but rather "Thou shalt commit no murder."

The second difficulty of this approach is the problem of "collision" when more absolutes than one are calling for allegiance in the same situation. Situations can easily be imagined, or documented from history, in which it is evidently necessary to choose between not lying and not taking life or between not taking one life and not defending another. The concept of absolute principle does not suffice here.

Still another shortcoming is the negative form which such absolutes almost inevitably must take. Very easily the effort to respect such prescriptions becomes transformed into a search for moral purity for its own sake, rather than an expression of love of the neighbor. It is possible to be very scrupulous about not taking life, and yet lack insight into the positive obligations which flow from a genuine respect for that same life.

Nevertheless, in the serious ethical decision-making process the language of absolute obligation, whatever its practical and philosophical shortcomings, is still the clearest language we have. The burden of proof still lies with those who claim that it is possible to have a community of moral discourse without certain shared understandings which function somehow like "principles." When speaking to the individual's decision-making in a given context, the situation-ethicists have much that is wholesome to say about flexibility, about the importance of loving motivation, and about the uniqueness of each choice. But they say this to persons who have already acquired somewhere a set of understandings about what constitutes the neighbor's welfare, with which they can then afford to be flexible. They have not demonstrated how ethical decision can be the subject of *community* concern — in justifying or condemning choices, in nurturing the immature, in adjudicating conflicts between the differing demands of different loves, in aiding the individual to keep watch on his own hasty and unworthy loves for the sake of his longer-range and worthier love of neighbor — without recourse to principle.[14]

After all, any case that can be made *for* war also appeals to principles claiming to stand above the individual, and they are generally less flexible, less humane, and less moral than those appealed to against it. In the concrete conflict situation, it is over against other absolutes, equally blunt and oversimplified, that this one is to be weighed. Courage, comradeship, freedom, a particular preferred form of government, the direction of history, or the integrity of territory are all, when they become reasons for killing, just as "absolute" in their demands, and far less human or humane in the attitude they express. They are still more degrading than the pacifist absolutes when applied in legalistic, self-justifying, ways by the naive and those who are not equipped (as the situationist is) for the luxury of situationally anguished existential choices. These pagan absolutes function with the same logical weaknesses as those of the

Ten Commandments but are far less worthy of such respect. They are more rigid not only psychologically (who can argue with "better dead than red"?) but also institutionally; the provision for killing is self-authenticating and self-governing. The military establishment has to be code-bound in a way that the church may, but need not be.

"Thou shalt not kill" is, as an absolute, still immeasurably more human, more personalistic, more genuinely responsible than the competitive absolute, "Thou shalt not let Uncle Sam down" or "Thou shalt fight for freedom" or "Never give up the ship." As in the age of Abraham or Moses the blanket prohibition of killing freed the Hebrews from the scourge of infant sacrifice, so today such a person-centered absolute prohibition may well help free us from other idolatries.

IV.
The Pacifism
of Programmatic
Political Alternatives

"*Can men practice politics without
doing violence? The answer is an imperative: They must if humanity is to
live. The fact that some men can do so
is evident enough in the struggles of
a Hindu ascetic and a Swedish diplomat
to lay the basis for the hope that a
politics of revolution and peace is within
the grasp of many more. To face the
cost of such a politics, in the cross,
is to affirm simultaneously the resurrection of humanity that is its outcome.*"
— James Douglass, The Non-Violent Cross

"*We are not so mad as to think that
we shall create a world in which murder
will not occur. We are fighting for a
world in which murder will no longer
be legal.*" — Albert Camus

"*The only thing that's been a worse
flop than the organization of non-violence
has been the organization of violence.*"
— Joan Baez

34

When we speak here of the "political" we refer to positions being taken or advocated for governments. A political program does not begin with the individual and what he may or may not do but with the decisions which the government must make. When we refer to this political pacifism as "programmatic," we indicate that it proposes concrete plans and goals rather than contenting itself with generalizations or condemnations. A programmatic political pacifism will propose for general adoption the banning of nuclear tests, the strengthening of the United Nations, or progressive disarmament. It provides intelligent and feasible solutions for problems which war does not solve. It assumes that there must be a solution to any political problem if competent political thought is directed to it. War is not such a solution to any problem. Measured by its worthy announced goals, war is counter productive. The statesman who resorts to war as an instrument of national policy is shortsighted and selfish. We need therefore to counteract his ignorance and selfishness by making available concrete suggestions which the statesman or his constituency can responsibly support.

This kind of programmatic pacifism was especially prevalent in Anglo-Saxon countries in the early 1930s. It was widely represented within the churches even though its reasoning was not narrowly religious in origin. On the level of popular acceptance, it largely collapsed in the later thirties with the rise of Hitler and has since been given little serious attention by mainstream figures. Its most consistent adversaries have been persons like Reinhold Niebuhr, who himself had

35

once held such a position.[15]

Some of the weaknesses of this position are minor and not constitutive. It is often taken by very naive people, whose calculation of what is politically possible is not based on realistic knowledge. Further, even if a position proposed from this perspective might be technically very possible and socially very desirable, it generally has little hope of commanding wide support from either the politicians currently in power or sufficiently wide segments of the population at large.

But there is another set of weaknesses which is deeper and more significant. This programmatic pacifism tends to misread the possibilities of wholesome social development. It places too much confidence in the efficacy of the methods it proposes; it counts too much on the goodwill of the parties in control. It thus may consider as feasible certain strategies which actually have no hope of effectiveness, however desirable their goals might be and however appropriate their methods taken in themselves might be.

By thus overestimating the likelihood of healthy solutions, this programmatic pacifism does not face outright the problem of failure. In its concern to propose a feasible alternative, does it concede to the power politicians their assumption that only guaranteed feasible alternatives are morally binding? Does it accept that morality should be tested by the promise of sure results? Does the tacit acceptance of such a test not open the door to violence after all? Or can the moral deed sometimes be the ineffective and costly thing? To face this latter challenge in a Christian way, pacifism needs a rootage in the meaning of the cross of Christ, which certainly was not a visibly effective strategy for reaching any worthwhile political goal.

Nevetheless, this sober pessimism about the usability of force and this creativity as to human solutions is what (all agree)[16] is needed in most societies, and even in most international conflicts, most of the time. Differing therein from the utopian or sectarian forms of pacifism, as well as from the utopian claims of militarism (see below), programmatic pacifism does accept the challenge of realism and relevance. It makes cogent its condemnation of trust in weapons by arguing that without weapons one could meet some of the same needs and achieve some worthy ends. It does not abandon society to the condemnation which it expresses over against the world's militarism.

It can afford, as the alternatives cannot, to be sober about the destructive potential, the likelihood of failure to achieve the set goals, which is inherent in the appeal to arms (every war has a loser on one side and sometimes both lose, when measured by the beginning goals). By not resorting to the simple solution of violence and thereby cutting short the creative search for real solutions, it forces itself to stay by the problem until another way through is found.[17]

If the claims of this programmatic approach are to be given a fair hearing, then we must project applications which would draw on the same resources in money, planning, and potential sacrifice of life which war can claim. "Nonviolence has never worked" is not a logically honest conclusion when there has never been a serious mobilization for it, with planning, strategy thinking, and education like that the military does, with budget for strategic studies and training, with investment in building skills and *esprit de corps,* and with readiness to sacrifice lives in the struggle.[18] When measured by such a fair test, in proportion to the cost of military methods in preparation and in lives, if there were such a thing as a calculus of units-of-justice-per-cost-in-persons, it could certainly be argued that history's few, hastily projected and poorly supported specimens of the nonviolent defense of justice have been no worse failures than the comparable violent alternatives.

After all, the only alternative which most societies face is an equally programmatic political militarism, which has all the same logical shortcomings.[19] Militarism too places enormous trust in the good intentions and righteousness of its own leaders. Often the non-pacifist accuses the pacifist of being "optimistic" or "unrealistic" about sin; but it is the military strategy which makes the most sweeping assumptions about the righteousness of one's own leaders; about their capacity to resist the temptations of power, about the quality of their control of their subordinates, and about their wisdom.[20] Militarism, just as much as pacifism, misreads the possibility of achieving its goals by the use of its means. Especially it misreads the significance of such labels as "freedom" or "victory" when these are identified as goals of immediate action.

A Semantic Parenthesis

Within the realm of programmatic pacifism some

38

distinct variations can usefully be identified, which may be worthy of separate attention. But before proceeding to such a selective catalogue of subtypes, we need to give some attention to a question of logic, or of conversational procedure, underlying the whole debate. It usually is assumed in conversations like this that the definitions we use should properly be borrowed from the non-pacifist mainstream. It tends to be assumed that the framework of moral thought is the same: that the values to be sought and the facts with which we begin are the same and the pacifist differs *only* in the rejection of certain kinds of means. The question is the same but the answer is different: the given quantities are the same but the conclusions to be reached are different.

Creative pacifist political critique will hasten to point out that there is no ground for such an assumption that the categories of analysis dictated by the non-pacifist traditions are adequate. The pacifist does not simply give a minority answer to the majority question; he challenges the propriety or the utility of the question itself. Two examples must suffice:

A. It is widely agreed that the use of the "sword," or the ultimate capacity to appeal to the power to coerce is the definition *sine qua non* of the state. If there is no coercive power there is anarchy. Over against this kind of definition the political pacifist will argue that the police power is not the center but the far edge, the *ultima ratio* of any wholesome human community. The health and in fact the very existence of a community depends upon maintaining the latency of

39

that power. If it is used often that civilization is less healthy; if it is used all the time that civilization is undergoing tyranny or anarchy. Anarchy is the presence of too much coercive power, not too little. Without risking the affirmation that there can be ordered societies without any *potential* recourse to some coercion, the practical pacifist will point out that there already have been and are societies where that ultimate recourse practically never needs to be used or never needs to be legally institutionalized ahead of time.

B. Another widespread axiom is that all "power" is ultimately of the same quality. The differences between the unspoken social pressures of the closed rural community and the outward coercion of urban police are only matters of degree. The difference between the police function and international war are again differences only in degree. It is thus inconsistent for the pacifist to reject war unless he also rejects police, or to reject killing by police if he is still willing to spank his children.

Now pacifists do vary in their views on spanking children; but practical pacifists all agree that it is simply silly to avoid recognizing the very significant qualitative differences distinguishing several kinds of power. "Power," even if it be called "coercive," is of a personal, humane, kind as long as the individual toward whom it is directed is conceived of as a person and his life is protected. The pressures of education, gossip, excommunication, or ostracism are still personal and permit the one against whom they are directed to be restored to the community. This personal quality may perhaps be retained by some exercise of "police power"; it certainly is abandoned in some other kinds of policing and utterly forsaken in war. To argue that "the problem of power is all of one piece" is possible logically, but it gives the common abstraction "power" priority over more significant variables. It is something like saying it is inconsistent for humans to practice contraception if they don't keep their dandelions from breeding, since "the problem of sexual reproduction is all of a piece." The alternatives may be arranged in the following way.

A. Responsible Appeasement

The word "appeasement" has been almost unspeakable since 1938, when it became the specific label for the acceptance by Britain and France of Hitler's annexation of Czechoslovakia. Yet the root meaning of the term points to what all good government does most of the time, namely to accept the sacrifice of what would be ideally desirable rather than fight a war about it. In every case where such a sacrifice works and it is possible to avoid hostilities, this approach is agreed by all to have been right.

It is *axiomatic* for this view — an axiom well documented from experience and still better from contemporary projections — that war, at least modern war, is worse than any other evil which can befall a society. Even when one possesses no immediate plan for achieving all one's desirable purposes, war should still be renounced, for it will not achieve them either. Thus those sacrifices, even tragic ones, which keeping the peace may impose are still preferable to the massive destruction and the hatefulness between peoples which a war causes. Such a willingness to accept losses and sacrifices, which may be great, but are still less than the losses imposed by war, is simply a logical application of the same process of calculating lesser evils which was always appealed to in favor of war when it was less destructive.

The one type of case in which it could be agreed that appeasement is wrong, and then of course it is very wrong (by programmatic political standards), is the case where the aggressor is not satisfied with the concession made to him, but is thereby only encouraged to become more disorderly and demanding. If his ultimate designs for world conquest are such that it seems nothing will stop him but war, then politicians responsive to majority opinion may conclude that it only makes things worse to postpone by concessions the confrontation which seems sure to come.

Nevertheless, the assumption that war is the only and always the better alternative to that particular kind of concessions is not (in real experience) the result of a rational and carefully calculating objective balancing of all the real political possibilities. This assumption, which has given the word "appeasement" a bad sound in the past decades, is imposed on the 1938 Munich agreement from within the history as it is read after the event by the winning party. It is a logical interpretation only *if* we take for granted in the given case that the aggression lies clearly only on one side and righteousness on the other and only *if* it is furthermore established that the particular kind of aggressive intention of the other party is such that it will be increased rather than decreased by having another territory to govern. The more carefully one develops the case for intervention which could be made for 1938, the more clear it becomes that such arguments could apply in very few other situations.

But more important is that we recognize that only the *winning* party can ever make this case for war rather than appeasement. The loser in any war would have always been better off to make his peace sooner rather than later, even against an absolutely unjust aggressor, as the experience of Denmark and the Low Countries in World War II or the Czechs in 1968 demonstrated. Their capacity to resist and later to rise up again was greater precisely because they accepted defeat soon enough that their society remained intact.

After all, if appeasement is to be condemned for failing to sate an aggressor's appetite, armed defense as well would have to be condemned for the far more frequent cases where it has touched off a wider conflagration, or failed seriously to slow down the aggressor. Appeasement can have failed monumentally once and still be preferable, on balance, as a general strategy.

All of the hindsight which has been used to argue that the Second World War would have been more efficient if it had begun in 1938, whatever the portion of truth in such a prediction, avoids asking whether the war, when it was undertaken, did what it was supposed to do. It stopped the spread of tyranny in Western Europe, but at the cost of giving the other half of Europe to Stalin. It did not save Poland for democracy nor save the lives of the Jews. The more anyone argues a particular case for the particular allied intervention of 1938, the more one must appeal to arguments and calculations which might in many other cases point in the other direction, thus demonstrating that in such other cases appeasement or, to use less tainted terms, conciliation and compromise, would be the responsible thing to do.

Our reference to the case of Munich should remind us of the special way in which the analogy proclaimed in the late 1960s by the U.S. State Department between Munich and Vietnam has served to blur the vision of many. "Never-another-Munich" has turned out to be a singularly unstatesmanlike case of misplaced moral absolution.

Not only must armed defense be tested by its inability to stop the aggressor; it also appeases. What were Franklin D. Roosevelt's agreements with Joseph Stalin if not "appeasement" on the other side? In return for the support of a tyrant the U.S. not only did not stop him but in fact conceded to him control over nearly half of Europe. The allies, in order to win a war, gave away to totalitarianism far more territories and populations that didn't belong to them than Munich gave to Hitler. In general, the military alliance is a far less discriminating kind of appeasement than the peacetime concession.

B. The Sobriety of Prudential Calculation

Somehow the debate about war often gets turned so as to make it seem that the pacifist is the one who by commitment to inflexible principle refuses to calculate effectiveness and the chances of happy solutions. Yet the argument is not only possible but quite cogent which faces the challenge of prudential calculation, and argues carefully that sobriety about the effects of violence must itself be part of the calculation justifying resort to violence. The evil of violence corrupts even the relatively righteous intentions of the relatively less guilty party to a social conflict. Even if we grant that in a given conflict one party is significantly more righteous than the other, or his cause more just, the very weapons he will resort to, once he has determined that violence is justified, will largely throw away that moral advantage. The good which is predicted does not come as a result of the war; evils which were not foreseen do actually arise, partly as a result of the very weapons used and partly because of the moral effect upon the more righteous party of his absolutizing his own relative righteousness into an authorization to destroy the adversary.

Reinhold Niebuhr has described as "irony" this characteristic of the historical process which generally produces results different from those by which decisions were thought to have been justified. That events should be impossible to predict with *such* certainty that moral choices can be made by reasoning back from the predicted outcomes, only stands to reason in a universe in which the centers of decision-making are multiple. When the historical process is conceived as a model machine where one person pushes the buttons or even as a nation with a single

45

capital, then to make decisions on the grounds of the simple choice between ultimate outcomes has a certain logic, even though already here it pretends to a utopian degree of omniscience. But when multiple other decision-makers are trying to do the same thing, each with a different set of goals, a different set of assumptions about the rules of the whole game and a different set of expectations about how they expect the other partners of the game to play, it is a mathematical certainty that none of the options among which we claim to be choosing can come to pass.

It is *axiomatic* for this position that the essence of political sobriety is coming to terms with the fact that the problem is man himself, and the way his reading of the facts and his description of his decisions is warped by his pride. Pragmatism will then be concerned not so much with piling up power and pulling strings as with expecting less and working more modestly, calculating more realistically the limits of the attainable, and then letting that sobriety feed back into a powerful skepticism about righteous causes which can justify the use of destructive instruments.

This kind of modestly prudential pacifism can never solve a problem or prove a point with absolute certainty. It is impossible to demonstrate as an *absolute* generalization that the evil tools to which he resorts will *always* and *completely* corrupt the one who uses them. In a world of relative good and relative evil it might well be — though it could never be provable — that in a particular case a relatively more wise use of a small, successful war by the relatively more unselfish party might do relatively less harm in the long run than at least the alternative which he thought of as an alternative.

Nevertheless, this kind of sober, prudential pacifism is the wisest and most honest view of the political scene available. It combines sobriety about one's own, and one's nation's, capacity for moral restraint with realism about the capacity of coercive instruments to attain valuable goals. In order to state the argument of prudential pacifism, it suffices to have demonstrated — and this is a demonstration in pure logic, not only in statistical probability — that it can *not* be assumed to have been *proved* in *advance most* of the time that projected results can justify a given destructive behavior in a game with several players. But not only in logic is the proof inconclusive; the record likewise denies everyone's pretentions to determine the course of history by pushing in the right direction.[21]

After all, the alternative strategy can never prove its projections absolutely either. Both in the record and in the theoretical contemplation of the dynamics of social change, the assumption that stronger arms in the hands of good guys are by prudential calculation likely to produce the desired outcomes has a still smaller probability.

47

V.

The Pacifism of Nonviolent Social Change

> *"The power at the disposal of a nonviolent person is always greater than he would have if he were violent. There is no such thing as defeat in nonviolence."*
> — *Mohandas K. Gandhi*

Every theology makes some room for the calculation of how most properly to achieve desired ends and prevent undesirable outcomes. In some ethical systems the calculation of effects is a minor consideration helping only to choose between available permissible ways of applying unchanging principles. In other cases the concept of effectiveness takes over completely the field of ethical deliberation and there is an explicit avowal of the place of such calculations in all decisions.

Now that the experience of Gandhi and Martin

Luther King has demonstrated that in some kinds of situation nonviolent methods can effectively bring about social change in the desired direction, it is appropriate for both these types of ethical thought, those for which effectiveness is the final consideration and those for which it is considered only instrumentally, to take account of this new information.[22]

Nonviolence as a tool of social change, in particular contexts, has some very decided advantages. It can be used by the poor and weak. It gives moral dignity to those who commit themselves to this discipline, a dignity which itself makes the action worthwhile even if the effort to change society is not immediately successful. The renunciation of violence robs the oppressor and the adversary of a pretext for resorting to even greater injustice.

This is a method which holds out special promise in areas where other methods have demonstrated their inability to help. In Latin America, for instance, the formula of "revolution" has been tested so often that no one can trust it. Not only has it not helped to change the basic social structures, but the polarization of Latin America under the anti-communist surveillance of the United States means that even if the internal conditions of a country were such that a revolution of violent character had some chance of success, the intervention from the North would make it impossible. This is just one sample of the kind of situation in which nonviolent methods of social change can demonstrably be effective.

It is *axiomatic* for this view that it is ultimately in everyone's interest for society to move in the direction of greater justice, and that the oppressor can be brought to see this by the application of pressures which respect his own humanity and open a way to change without too much loss of "face." It reckons soberly with the reticence of most men to refrain from evildoing unless they are assured that at least some of their goals can be reached without it, and it provides a better path to those goals. It reckons realistically with the improbability that "purely moral" considerations (in the forms listed in I and II above) will convince many people. Just as politically programmatic pacifism provides alternative possibilities in international affairs, so this position seeks alternatives to the attitudes and the social structures which make men ready for war.

This pacifism with its promises of effectiveness has real weaknesses. It is effective when one can appeal to the conscience of the oppressor, as with Gandhi in India appealing to British self-respect, or the American Negro appealing to the U.S. Constitution. Can it be effective against sadists and brutes? Can it be effective against a regime in which oppression is carried on with a good conscience? Can it maintain its conviction for months or years without any visible success?

The professional ethical theorist will point out that this kind of pragmatic nonviolence mixes two kinds of thought. Does it really claim that violence is always wrong, or only that it is usually unwise and ineffective? If the advocate of nonviolence promises success, does this mean that violence would be justified after all if nonviolence were not successful? If on the other hand it does appeal to a "moral absolute" or "higher law" in its rejection of violence, how seriously do we need to take its claim that it will always be effective within the attainable future? By not forsaking the claim to success, it may remain an expression of selfishness, especially if practiced by a whole class, race, or social group.

Especially in its modern form, in which nonviolent techniques have been elaborated quite apart from spiritual disciplines, nonviolence is not in any way specifically Christian. In fact some have argued that it might be most congenial to the non-Western personality, which is more inured to suffering and less oriented toward either comfort or self-fulfillment, than is Western "Christian" man.

Nevertheless, nonviolent action remains the only accessible recourse for the oppressed, and a most serious one in some circumstances for the morally responsible minority (who would have other ways of speaking), but for whom nonviolent means offer a meaningful adjunct to their more traditional processes of opinion formation and political decision.

After all, the honest application of any of the above critical considerations would condemn war even more. War also mixes claims of absolute obligation for which it is better to die, with claims of pragmatic effectiveness which permit acceding a reasonable peace when one is losing. War as well is demoralizing when it is unsuccessful; war as well is most ineffective when the adversary is irrational or brutal in his commitment to violence. Certainly war is not a specifically Christian ethical strategy either. Even if one could claim that the soldier's selfishness is not categorically worse in

51

inward moral quality than the selfishness of the nonviolent crusader, it is profoundly different for the victim.

VI.

The Pacifism of Prophetic Protest

"How, they asked, could I be calm about a six-year sentence for pouring blood on draft records? ... I had thoroughly considered the possible consequences before choosing civil disobedience twice."
— *Philip Berrigan from prison 1968*

Some of the positions described above have concentrated on whether the individual makes himself guilty of sin, before his conscience or before what he understands to be the moral law, by participating in a war. More of them have asked whether he places himself on the wrong side of the course of history, contributes to the wrong chain of causes and effects.

But it is also possible, especially in certain extreme situations, to let one's behavior be dictated not by considerations of "right and wrong" in either of these accustomed senses, but rather by a concern to communicate. For example: some income tax objectors intend to prevent any dollars that were in their hands from ever getting into the hands of the Pentagon. They are concerned for moral integrity, for having nothing to do with the whole business. Others, however, make no such claim. They admit their inability to keep dollars away from Caesar whose superscription they carry, but still they do not voluntarily pay all their taxes. They are trying to "make a point." Then their decision about an action is not weighed only by whether as a deed it is permitted or forbidden by the law of God or by love, but also by what it *says* at a given point. One wants to *say* something about American society or about colonialism or about the race issue; but the only way you can "say" this is to do something. This kind of consideration would apply not only to marches and demonstrations and vigils, or to symbolic token actions like tax refusal; it could also apply to a refusal to accept the draft card or a weapon.

It is *axiomatic* for this view that thought and action, word and deed are inseparable. Man is a meaning-monger whether he speaks or not. Every action is a word, and often the unspoken word is louder; sometimes the unreflective, acted-out thought is more genuine, or more logical, than the abstraction.

Since this position is motivated by considerations extrinsic to the action itself, to evaluate it ethically is most difficult. To interpret an act as communication we would ask whether what it says is true and necessary, and how clearly and surely the message is carried. Usually this will be asked
54

from the perspective of the "audience" aimed at. Yet sometimes it is to oneself that one must prove something: a duty to one's own integrity demands an act of disavowal. This is not necessarily a selfish or self-righteous stance; it may be the only way to state the absoluteness of the moral law, that one says one rejects what it rejects, without calculating one's chances of getting away with it or of achieving a change in public policy.

Often the gestures of protest bear a message which is at the same time founded in one of the other types of pacifism of which we have spoken; then they do not stand alone but are a particular publicity tool. The parabolic deed can, however, become a type of its own in that:

— an absolutist judgment against a particular war may for instance be taken without being subject to the test of whether it would apply in the same way to all other possible wars. The visceral-dramatic dimension can make categorical the present rejection of a particular evil, without rooting it in a philosophically generalized ethic. One can thus make very clear how much one cares; at the cost, of course, of not saying very clearly why.

— war may only be the last straw in one's mounting rejection of a racist, exploitative, dehumanizing "system." Without a systematic ethical answer on war itself, one concludes "this is too much!" and fixes on war, one point where the character of the "system" is preeminently visible, to draw the line.

— war itself is seen as dramatic communication. One asks not only whether killing is wrong, but what war *says:* to one's own people, to the "enemy" population, to world opinion — about political and human values.

— war is arrogance, in that a given nation (or rather, a clique of rulers within a given nation) will presume to impose its vision of the future on the rest of the world, claiming some moral right or duty by virtue of its own power, success, or philosophy.

— war is idolatry, in that it makes of the welfare and the decisions of one's own nation an ultimate value to which if necessary all else must be sacrificed.

In these several ways, the necessity of a dramatic, corporally visible "No!" can be perceived in a self-evident way without the protestor's sensing any need to support his rejection either with general lines of reasoning or with alternative courses of action. The rejection of the present evil is valid for its own sake, and this must be *said* by word *and deed* whether there is another visible option or not.

This position has very serious intellectual and ethical disadvantages. By bringing into play a number of additional variables for the evaluation of an action, which is no longer simply a contribution to the social process, but also a confession of faith, a sermon, and an anathema, it makes it much more difficult for any given action to have the same meaning for all involved, more difficult for a whole group to take a common position without regimentation.[23] Yet at the same time that the choice is made more complex, this kind of declamatory action demands a powerful sense of moral certainty. Self-righteous claims to some kind of unique prophetic authority are almost necessarily implicit when one takes such a stance. Yet such arrogance is also a kind of violence.

Nevertheless the perception of the moral meaningfulness of deeds, with which this stance begins, is correct. The conformity of the masses is a powerful word of support for present policies; vocal dissent is of little weight, if not linked with dissenting action. The negative vote which goes no further than voting is one kind of dissenting voice; the refusal to cooperate with the majority decision is a voice of another magnitude. Especially in our age of verbal hyperalimentation where the ears and the brain sift out much they hear and the memory drops most of what was read, the amplifier which the acted word becomes is the only way for some messages to be heard.

After all, it is usually, often to an even greater degree, characteristic of war that it purposes to "say" something, and that concern for that "meaning" complicates its moral evaluation. The youth who enlists is often trying to say something to himself or his parents about his growing up; bearing arms is a demonstration of virility or dependability. Nationally, as the Vietnam case illustrates dramatically, the recourse to war or the insistence on staying in a war may be motivated not by the political ends to be sought in themselves, by the repulsion of aggression or the possibility of setting up a peaceful order, but rather by the desire to communicate to others that we will not be pushed around or that we are people who keep our promises, or that communist aggression does not pay. The "communication" by killing is even less clear and even harder to make a moral case for. It differs from the nonviolent types of protest in that the enemy, the victim, can never be the one to whom one communicates. To the extent to which the warlike action is successful, it can communicate only to another "public"; we crush *Vietnam* for the sake of what must be proved to the Chinese or the Russians or the Burmese about the American character, whereas nonviolent "demonstration" seeks to communicate to the one to whom it is *addressed*, and whom it inconveniences.

VII.
The Pacifism of Proclamation

"As she encountered this call historically, not only in Jesus' words, but in His death and resurrection, so also the church can make this message effectual only by passing it along in her deeds of authentic witness."
— *Hans-Werner Bartsch*, Communio Viatorum

All of the positions sketched above have rooted their ethical thought in some conception of righteousness. Ethics is seen as an expression of concern for the integrity of a person in his decisions, or for the propriety of an act as seen in its corresponding with the demands of the law, or the rightness of an act as seen in its social effects.

But by concentrating on these dimensions, as Christian ethics has largely done for centuries, we have missed another major dimension of Christian concern, one which is especially vital

59

in the New Testament and which increasingly came to be seen as central in the essence of the Protestant Reformation and in the missionary vision of the church.

This missing element is the understanding of the total Christian life as an aspect of the proclamation of the kingdom of God. Jesus, like His predecessor John, certainly understood His very being and not only His words as a living sermon. Jesus' words were proclamation but so were His healings and His exorcisms, His very presence.

This centering of ethical concern into proclamation constitutes the unfinished business of the Reformation. The Reformation reoriented exegesis and the sacraments around the concept of proclamation and increasingly penetrated dogma and missionary thought from this perspective; but it never succeeded in thinking of Christian *behavior* as proclamatory or kerygmatic.

If ethics can be illuminated from the kingdom message it will break the bounds of the other views. An ethic of law or of effects or of personal integrity is an ethic which enables man to be righteous. One can plan one's behavior and interpret God's demands in such a way that the right action is feasible. But so to tailor one's understanding of God's demands that one is sure to be able to meet them is already pharisaism.

The proclamation that the kingdom of God is at hand gives us a new criterion of possibility. We henceforth cease to calculate what is normally, humanly feasible. We no longer resign ourselves to less than the best.

The proclamation of the kingdom is at the

same time a new criterion of righteousness. That action is good which communicates to my neighbor the coming of the kingdom for him. Beyond this, proclamation is a new criterion of the center of Christian truth: the coming of the kingdom means that God has now made me really to be the servant of my neighbor.

Ethics in the New Testament reflects this "proclamatory" mood in the way it mixes prediction and promise in its commands. It is impossible to distinguish "you are" and "you shall" and "you ought." Christian obedience is not derived from calculation of how to meet requirements in order to receive rewards; it is the working out of one's life in a new divinely decreed context. Now in the case of war it is the enemy (since it is with him I am asked to deal) who is the neighbor I am to love. My action must be such as to communicate or proclaim to him the nature of God's love for him. It might be possible to argue that this could be done with a certain kind of force, moral or social or even physical, but certainly it cannot be said by threatening or taking his life.

Underlying this approach is *the Protestant axiom* that the proclamation of the Word of God is the true motor of history and the locus of its meaning. It is not the business of Christian obedience to protect or improve upon this word, to filter it or support it or bend it to fit cases and possibilities, but simply to speak it and to live from faith in its finality.

"The Sermon on the Plain proclaims salvation unconditionally, without respect for human possibility. Christians experienced this proclamation

61

historically in the encounter with the risen Lord, in that through this encounter the rescuing of the lost by God's intervention was attested. Now the church passes on this same assurance in her own preaching. But just as this affirmation historically came to the church not only in the word of Jesus but in His death and resurrection, so she can pass on this proclamation with historic effectiveness only by behavior which has the character of a witness. Because the attesting of salvation is not a supplemental assignment, which is added as a second requirement to that of the acceptance of salvation, but because the acceptance of salvation itself only occurs in the act of the testimony which passes it on, therefore the church, to the extent to which she is true to the church of Jesus Christ, which names Jesus as Lord, is directed to the neighbor. The social significance of the church is given in her commission to witness, because this commission necessarily includes behavior toward the neighbor."[24]

This kind of position has serious weaknesses especially when we seek to commend it to non-Christians or Christians of quite other traditions. It is most clearly and convincingly stated in the writings of a few Lutheran theologians[25] and is most at home in the Lutheran context. European Protestant thought has been compelled by Karl Barth to let theology as a "science," *i.e.*, as an intellectual discipline with its own intrinsic dignity, define its own terms and refuse to be judged by the assumptions of any other intellectual approach. It has been conditioned as well by the heritage of Rudolf Bultmann, who in an equally unaccountable way locates the meaning of reality in an inexplicable self-awareness of one's identity. Thus continental neo-Protestant thought is quite able to conceive of normative Christian proclamation as setting its own terms, as making demands *sui generis* which need not and in fact cannot be tested by the standards of any other stance. This is not proud solipsism; it is an extremely humble position. It denies to the theologian as intellectual the right to call God to account for the strangeness of His ways of speaking, and refuses to the thinker the license to improve and adapt God's message. But in conversation with other Christian traditions, and especially in conversation with the world, and with other disciplines, this kind of insistence upon stating Christian proclamation in the right and not the wrong terms, and demanding that we think in a new mode of thought because the gospel demands it, is perceived as a kind of provincial pride.

It is thus a further shortcoming of this position that since it affirms the unconditional possibility of proclaiming love to the neighbor, and makes this statement without reference to cases and details, it provides no very clear guidance for the case-by-case decisions which we do have to keep on making. Shall a proclamatory pacifism always seek neutrality in every political conflict or can it take sides nonviolently? Can it even accept that one kind of violence is less evil than another? The statement that it is precisely the enemy who is the neighbor I am to love, and the statement that the coming of the kingdom of God makes all things new, do not immediately answer that question. Is this "Word" then not

63

an abstraction? Does it not after all fail to communicate, i.e., to be Word, when "my action proclaims God's unmerited love for the Godless?" is set up as an ethical guide?

Nevertheless, this is the Protestant axiom. It is true that Jesus' deeds, especially His dealings with sickness and with foreigners, and with hunger and with violence, have a "word" dimension. It is correct that freeing ethics from pharisaism would be a consistent prolongation of Luther's freeing justification from works.

After all, as we have just seen in a wider context, war also proclaims an understanding of God and how He deals with sinners. Especially when it is said that war is being prepared for or carried on in the name of peace or freedom, or to teach the world a lesson, it always does communicate a message about whether we think the people we are dealing with are objects of the love of God or not. In the modern world every war proclaims something about man and usually also something about race and wealth.

As long as most Christians and most military agencies do not build a clear casuistic fence to identify the limits of their use of violence — and generally they have not done so — then all militarism is likewise running away from serious casuistic discipline and taking refuge in unaccountable abstract proclamations of virtue.

Parenthesis: Program and Practicality

The "varieties" dealt with thus far have all taken seriously in one way or another the challenge of "program," i.e., they are ready to write a recipe for society, though they vary in the ways in which they found, or motivate, their opposition to war. Yet there is a very significant variation along another scale to which we have not yet paid attention: how closely does practice need to follow the prescription? For some, the mere possession of an alternative vision includes an immediate obligation to lobby or propagandize for that policy; for others this does not follow at all necessarily. Such variations would apply within most of the types of thought identified above. We pause here for a sketchy kind of catalogue.

A. How Practical Must You Be?

1. There are those for whom a practical alternative must, by definition, be one which can win acceptance and actually be applied. The advocacy of the alternative is then not complete until, through all the channels of due process, the rudder of state can be turned. "Practical" then means not only that the policy, *if* applied, would resolve the international problems; it means also that the policy must be one which can win acceptance by the people, or at least by the people in power.

2. There are those who reckon seriously with the same obligation of efficacy, yet who recognize that "the system" is so corrupted by hidden interests and lines of power that it will never do the right thing of its own accord. There is, however, the extreme recourse of civil disobedience, conceived as an emergency appeal from due process to the consciences of men; of those in office or of the public. Suffering and shock, it is hoped,

will reach where letters to journals and statesmen cannot. The objector, though disobedient, remains within the limits of submission and accepts his punishment.

3. Lying somewhere between these first two forms is the civil disobedience of the test case. It may be seen either as a most extreme form of due process or as a most modest form of civil disobedience. Which it will be is decided not by the dissenter but by the system. Here one appeals not to men's consciences but rather to another branch of government; against the excesses of the executive or the impotence of the legislature, one appeals to the courts. If sustained by the courts, the test case has been a successful experience of due process. If not sustained, then one is in the posture of civil disobedience, but one's claim that the law one broke was unjust has been somewhat weakened by the effort to prove one's innocence.[26]

4. Still more critical of "the system" is what has been called (in a shift of the meaning of the adjective) "uncivil" disobedience. One no longer believes that the consciences of men can be appealed to; yet a minority can force its will on the majority, can obtain negotiation leverage, if it is willing to jeopardize property, to block the normal functioning of civil administration, the economy and the university, and to run the risk of violence, though not intending to kill. The claim to programmatic effectiveness is upheld, but the goal set can be achieved only coercively, by forcing someone to back down. If one does not succeed, the effect is generally to harden the adversary's resolve. Both the advocates of racial

justice and the critics of the Vietnam war began acting in this spirit in the U.S. in 1967.

B. How Real Is the Option?

The spectrum drawn above (in order of increasing alienation) progresses in the degree of opposition to the authorities but retains the claim to be justified by one's chances of bringing about the results sought. There is, however, a different line along which it is possible to vary in the way one interrelates feasibility and responsibility.

1. The claim to present a practical alternative may be quite clear and concrete, as it often is with Quaker study documents. The path suggested is one which could really be taken, starting from here, if one wished.

2. On the other hand it is also possible to retain the claim that a given international conflict *could have been* resolved, as a description of the international scene, but not concede that one's right to uphold this claim is tested by whether one can bring rulers or population to practice it. "You could have done otherwise" may clothe a word of prophetic condemnation, needing to be proclaimed as a denunciation of idolatry in the full awareness that men will not repent, or that it is too late for repentance to save them. "You need not be the slaves of the vicious circle of violence" may be a gospel invitation which a few will hear even as the unheeding masses rush on. "You will be sorry you chose this path" may be a warning which will, later, enable some to find the grace of repentance. In any of these contexts, the practicable yet unpractical programmatic

option finds its relevance not as a real path we may take tomorrow but as a way to clothe the call to reconciliation in the success-centered mythic language of our time.

3. In still another way one can contemplate practical options without needing to be able to implement them. They may be pedagogical paradigms, ways of testing one's thought patterns, techniques to clarify logical options. One may look at pragmatic options in order to undercut the non-pacifist's claim that he is a realist and the pacifist is utopian; or as a way of entering conversation with those whose habits of thought are limited to short-range ends-means calculations,[27] even while one's own position is not limited to or judged by such criteria. "War is not a usable instrument; there would be other ways" protects the pacifist against the accusation that he does not care, or that he does not deal with reality, yet without committing him to "deliver" a nonviolent solution which actually can win acceptance.

The strategic difference between these positions has been publicly debated in recent years in such close linkage to the issues of Vietnam and race that for many observers these complexities are a peculiar burden of the concerns of peace and racial justice. For some the resulting debates among pacifist and race-relations agencies, may seem even to discredit the pacifist concern. This is a wrong reading of the facts. These variations are visible around the peace issue because it is an important issue; but the same set of problems in instrumentation would have to be faced if we were concerned about contraception or prohibition, the single tax or Keynsian economic controls, urban transportation or guaranteed income as moral issues. The same variations in degrees of real practicality apply just as well in the military realm. They plague the strategy thought of the white citizens' councils as much as they do that of the civil rights movements.

VIII.

The Pacifism of Utopian Purism

"There is no way to peace: peace is the way."
— A. J. Muste

There is presently a much greater awareness and recognition, than a decade ago, that the New Testament style of discourse — and the recent language of counter culture — is not culturally or morally irrelevant. It can stand over against pragmatism as a credible alternate vision of the relationship between the good and the real. In addition, it exposes the contradiction in means and ends of those who cast aside the good in order to accomplish it.[28]

A society which hates its enemies and which, although it says killing is wrong, punishes its killers by killing them — thereby telling them that they were right — is so twisted that it is unworthy of defense. We cannot get from here to the Holy City by compromise or by calculated risks but only by a leap of faith.

The people who claim to be relevant, and claim to be able to measure out their creativity and their courage in small doses, so as not to be crucified, have not proved that their compromise increased their efficacy. A purely utopian ethic which seeks to be justified, not by its result, but by its purity, is, as far as we know, still just as efficient as one which seeks efficiency as a goal. Did not Jesus say that it was when we forsake all for the kingdom that everything else will be added to us? Did He not say as well by implication that those who seek first the other things will miss both the other things and the kingdom?

There is then no real reason for our rejection of war to need to be propped up either by considerations of how that rejection will itself improve the world, or by calculation of how our rejection can be made more responsible or acceptable by being made less consistent.

This position can be called a "purism" not because it lays claim to the purity of guiltlessness or perfect achievement, but because it demands a newness of relationships from which every justification of hostility has been banned. It is the demand of the categorical imperative: that my behavior be governed by the criterion that I must do only that which, if all men did it, would bring a new order.

It is *axiomatic* for this position that man is made for a city of love and that he cannot enter it through the gates of concession and compromise. He will have no rest until that city is realized. One gets there not by compromising with the present but by the confessing of a faith which makes the future real in symbolic ways today.

It is no argument against this position to say that it does not accept the criterion of responsibility, as long as it can argue in return that the criterion of responsibility itself becomes a self-justifying and ultimately self-defeating idolatry. It is not a position which will be very effective in winning respect of the typical Western man with his calculation of yield per unit of input; but is not that way of calculating already part of the sickness from which we are seeking to help modern man to leap free?

It is a disadvantage of this position that it seems, to those whom it condemns, to be of no assistance, to be another form of the monastic retreat, living parasitically on the very system which it rejects. If the ideal society stands only in a purely negative relationship to the society in which we live, where then do you get the ideal by which you judge? Which of the possible ideals from which one might judge the present is right and how do you know that? Do you not confirm the present system in its fallen implacability just as much by refusing to talk with it as by working with it?

The purist position can explain its refusals but not its continuities. The spirit of revolution cannot be institutionalized; if the "New Left" is around tomorrow it will be the old "New Left." The question raised by this position is not so much a flaw in its pacifism, its judgment on the evil powers of society, as in its wider vision of human nature, its trust in the goodness of the moral self.

Nevertheless utopias and apocalypses may be the most powerfully responsible instruments of change. A patient depth reading of history points in this direction. If, as Jesus says,[29] pragmatic utilitarianism is self-defeating because self-fulfillment is found only in self-forgetfulness, might there not be an analogy to this on the social-moral level? Might it not be that the most right action is the one most forgetful of its ramifications? That God's sovereignty might enter ethics at the point of denying His accountability to the prudential calculations of men of little faith?

After all, this utopian pacifism trusts less to an irrational leap of faith than does the rhetoric which tells us that by forcibly making refugees you are defending self-determination, or that by supporting a puppet government you are enabling democracy to grow. There is no more utopian institution than an idealistic war. The Atlantic Charter or the Wilsonian 14 points are utopian documents, no more responsibly meshed with the historical realities than is the vision of the New Jerusalem in Revelation 20. War is utopian both in the promises it makes for the future and in the black-and-white way of thinking about the present, especially about the enemy, which it assumes. The utopian character of war has been demonstrated repeatedly in the past century in the outworkings of the assumption that after having defeated the one bad nation the forces of good can go home. It is utopian in believing that there will ever be a world in which "world moral leadership" can be exerted by a nation whose overseas presence is predominantly commercial and military! It is utopian in that it continues to believe or at least to say that it believes that one can win a war without committing atrocities,

73

and that the only obstacle to peaceful settlement is the inexplicable obstinacy of the other side. In all these dimensions (speaking now for United States civilization) it is the purist vision, the product of the morality of the Western film, with the easily (ethnically.) identified good guys and bad guys, and the unlimited justification of violence in the hands of the good, which seems to be guiding United States policies overseas.

IX.

The Pacifism
of the
Virtuous Minority

*"The regenerated do not go to war
nor engage in strife. Spears and swords
of iron we leave to those, who, alas,
consider human blood and swine's blood
of well-nigh equal value."*
— Menno Simons, 1539.

*" . . . The church appreciates and
prays for the government. It also gives
to the government a clear testimony
as to its own convictions on war, but
there is no attempt to control the
government, and no demand that it
follow a given course with respect to
specific points of foreign policy. Its only
demands are those which the New
Testament directs to Christians themselves as regenerated members of the
kingdom of God."*
— Guy F. Hershberger, War, Peace,
and Nonresistance

Ever since Constantine, it is a normal reflex in everyone's ethical thought to assume that when we ask about right behavior we are seeking a standard to apply consistently to all men. It is always thought to be a fair test to ask, "What if everybody did this?" or "Can you ask this of everyone?" This line of thought generally supports the legitimation of war because of the self-evident need to save society and because of the unreadiness of many men to live sacrificially (that the sacrifices demanded by war are ultimately so much easier to make than those demanded by nonviolent love, and that war does actually save society, could also be plausibly doubted, but that argument is not our present concern).

But logic must call into doubt this axiom that ethics are for everybody. Within Roman Catholicism there is the ancient tradition of the "evangelical counsels," which hold up before men the call to a level of morality distinct from that of merely keeping the law, a level to which all men are invited but on which the religious are expected actually to be able to live. Within the pietist and Wesleyan traditions there is the concept of "Christian perfection," again a level of moral being, and performance derived from that level of being, which are not assumed to be given to or demanded of all men. Life on this level is precisely not a matter of demand but a very special gift.

Protestantism in general has not developed explicitly this kind of vision of a minority morality as it runs counter to some of the major emphases of the mainstream reformation. In practice, however, most Protestants do expect of their pastor and of the missionary a level of wholesomeness and unselfishness quite distinguishable from the kind of life which they assume the church has a right to ask of the rest of them.

In a different form, the ethic of the free church or believers' church tradition within Protestantism is likewise not an ethic for every man. Discipleship after the pattern of the manhood of Jesus may well be the calling of every man, be he Christian or not, be he aware of his calling or not; but that calling can only become a concrete expectation in the life of the individual and in the practice of the church if he has committed himself to a discipline in response to that call. The believers' church would hold that all Christians must be committed to full discipleship; but for those who cannot draw upon the resources of forgiveness and regeneration, the guidance of the Spirit and the counsel of the brethren, it is not meaningful to expect the same quality of life and is therefore improper to seek to enforce it. Christianity is for everybody; but Christian ethics is only for Christians.

This kind of minority morality had already made it clear in the middle ages that killing must be rejected for persons who live on the level of the gospel. In Catholic canon law it still applies to the cleric and the religious and is recognized in the laws of some states. It probably explains the cultural and emotional rootage of conscientious objector privileges in Western legal systems, even though these are then extended to persons who understand their position in other terms.

It is *axiomatic* for this view that morality finds

its context in a freely covenanted response to the call of God. In this joyful fellowship, life is freed from concern both for personal merit and for demonstrable results. Good is not what promises to move the world in the right direction. Good is that which, responding to the nature of God as He has graciously manifested Himself, participates already in the nature of that toward which the world must move.

Once morality is freed from the bind of needing to meet the test of applicability to all, we are for the first time able to look at the good action, at that deed which has about it the quality of conformity to the goodness of God, as a question distinct from judgmental casuistry. This is what is meant by our title's reference to the "virtuous" minority. Only if we recognize that ethics is not generalizable are we free to use in a wholesome way the concept of *virtue*, i.e., of goodness intrinsic in certain kinds of action or character. This pattern of thought is demanded by biblical language with its catalogues of virtues and vices. It is strongly supported not only by the tradition of monastic self-discipline but also by the stoic naturalism of modern man's self-cultivation. Violence is a vice to be avoided; nonviolence or meekness is a virtue and to be cultivated.

There are serious dangers in this type of minority pacifism. It may acquiesce in the compromises made by the majority, once it has withdrawn therefrom, and thereby undermine its claim to a hearing as critic. The monastic few may accept minority status as something to be proud of and set apart by rather than as a call to all men. This temptation is built-in especially if one develops a theory of two moral levels, an intentional double standard for clergy and laymen or for church and world. A quite analogous temptation besets the sectarian-protestant form of minority morality.[30] The minority can easily become ecumenically irresponsible, unconcerned for the needs or concerns or commitments of other Christians. It is possible for the search for a virtue not anchored pragmatically to become obscurantist, or self-centered and thereby self-righteous, seeking to save one's own soul by turning one's back on others, too easily reconciled to the inability of the minority to do any good in a wider world.

One normal implication of this minority stance is to approve by implication, for most men, the very position one rejects for oneself. The Catholic understanding of the monastic morality has no trouble with this; for the freely chosen "Rule" is not identified with everyman's moral obligation. Christians in the Historic Peace Churches, they are told, should also accept such minority status and be accepted in it; a special gadfly performance by virtue of which the rest of society is kept from being at peace with its compromises.

Such an understanding of a "vocational" role for the peace churches has been fostered by the relativistic or pluralistic mood of modern denominationalism, in which the question of objective right and wrong is relativized by the acceptance of a great variety of traditions, each having its own claims to truth arising out of its own history. Each may be recognized as having a *portion* of the truth, on condition that none impose his view on another. What in denominational pluralism arises out of democratic self-restraint, becomes in some contemporary Protestant theologies a committed relativism, founded in a view of truth as itself having no firm landmarks, but consisting in the interplay of several positions, several of which may be recognized as "valid" or "authentic" or "adequate" but none specifically as "true." It is in this spirit that many non-pacifists since the 1930s have been willing to grant to the pacifists a "prophetic" or "vocational" role, on condition that in turn they accept their always being voted down by those who have to do the real work in the world.

Such an acceptance of minority status is ultimately unsatisfactory because it concedes to the majority that *for the majority* the position of compromise is justified, and that a position faithful to the gospel cannot be practiced within real life. It further courts the danger of complacency or self-righteousness for the person or group taking the position which is acknowledged to be morally superior, at the same time that he is (or they are) released, under the mantle of mutual tolerance, from the discipline of seeking to commend his position effectively to others. In the experience of the peace churches, the "vocational" label is a cover for failing to decide how clear one is on one's own convictions and their relevance to one's brethren, while still taking credit for a righteous stance.

Nevertheless, the morality of the New Testament is a minority morality, and the same will be the case wherever the Christian church lives in genuine missionary nonconformity. The pacifism of the minority avoids the puritan legalism which would seek to impose upon all men a level of performance for which they do not have the spiritual or educational resources, as well as the latitudinarian legalism which spends its efforts planning pretexts for permitting almost anything because someone is going to have to do it anyway.

It is only in the minds of critics that the nonconformist minority has renounced social effectiveness. At least in certain times and places and ways, this stance is the presupposition of a meaningful communication. One excellent modern sample of this is the way in which Dorothy Day, the spirit at the heart of the *Catholic Worker*[31] movement, who for two generations has been the center of a movement of charity and social nonconformity with almost no settled constituency and no legal status, came to be listened to by the bishops at Vatican II simply because of the symbolic quality and integrity of her commitment.

After all, war has its own minority ethic, that of the SS or the Green Beret. Special military units, paratroopers and marines and commandoes of various kinds, Western movie and espionage heroes, have always been especially honored and publicly rewarded for practicing a morality which would not be tolerated within an orderly society. Certainly the spiritual danger of self-congratulation is no less in this case.

On the international scale, the vision of an elite calling has been applied just as proudly, and far more destructively, as a justification of war, than the pacifists' sense of privilege has ever been applied to their abstention from war. The Knights Templar and the Order of Malta, the white man's burden and the saving of Asia from communism have all justified war under the label of a unique righteous calling which other men or nations do not have.

X.

The Pacifism
of the
Categorical Imperative

*"The kingdoms of this world may be-
come the kingdom of the Lord and of
his Christ."*
— H. J. Cadbury

It seems practically self-evident to the average
Western mind that any ethical commitment can be
most usefully tested by the question: "What
happens if everybody does it?" In the heritage
of Christendom, it used to be realistic to assume,
when thinking about right and wrong, that everyone would be listening, i.e., that one was doing
the moral thinking for the whole of Western
Christian civilization, for whom the Christian
church was recognized as the authoritative moral
teacher. This called for every moral decision to
be evaluated by two tests, which usually coincide
but may be distinguished in their logic:

(a) What will happen if it becomes public

policy? What if the president would do this?

(b) What would happen if everybody did it?

We have referred earlier to the impact of this kind of assumption when it is linked with further pre-definitions of the goals which must be met by a public policy, or concerning the amount of unselfishness which can be expected of persons in large numbers or in large groups. This kind of logic leads to one of the most self-evident kinds of justification not only for violence but also for class and national egoism. For this reason we pointed out above that the assumptions of this Christendom logic of generalizability are by no means self-evident, and that it might be more appropriate to say that Christian ethics should seek to be able to meet the test of asking, "What will happen if *not* everyone does it?" and "What will happen if what Christians do is *not* public policy?"

But our pointer to the limits of the criterion of generalizability in moral logic should not be read as granting the claimed universality (and consequent legitimacy) of group selfishness. Nor should it be granted as proved that this Christendom mode of thought always works in favor of non-pacifist positions. Ever since Immanuel Kant, the imperative, "Act in the way you wish everyone would," has been meant to function not as a screen to filter out every idealism on the ground that not everyone is willing to share it, but rather as a prod to setting higher goals.

Its unspoken *axiom* has been that one of the safest ways to seek to stand in judgment upon my own propensities to selfishness is to posit other men, or all other men, as the agent; to ask how things would look if everyone else did what I contemplate doing.

If by "everyone" we mean not "the majority of people as they are now," but rather "our vision for the way the world should become," then we can understand much of the liberal and utopian pacifism of the 1930s in its most authentic light. Test how you want to behave by whether you would want to live in a world where everybody would act as you did. Would you want a world where every offense calls forth violent retaliation? where every prince and every parliament reserves the right of wrathful redress? If not, then you must make the renunciation of coercion and retaliation the law of your own community. If everyone in the U.S. were a conscientious objector, then, true enough, the American capacity to influence governments around the world would be much less, but so would the American crime rate, and it would at least be sure that American cities would never be destroyed by an atomic exchange nor by an invading army; and the funds and personnel available for influencing the world in peaceful ways and for healing our society would be increased by more than half the present federal budget. The hypothetical test is not a very probable one but it still makes a clear point.

This kind of reasoning is full of logical loopholes. As self-evident as it seems at first, it is not a very helpful kind of proof. The reminder that a society populated completely by conscientious objectors would have very little crime, no military expenditures, and large resources available for social welfare causes, simply serves to dramatize the limited usefulness of putting questions this way. To say that I would want to live in a world where everyone would treat me the way I would want to be treated may be a sign of psychological immaturity; it certainly has no direct relation to any questions we really ask or have any occasion to solve in concrete ethical decisions.

Nevertheless it would be irresponsible not to take some cognizance of the fact that in the Western world Christian moral thought does impinge on a large element of society, reaching well beyond the committed members of disciplined Christian communities. Christian appeals for international aid or for civil rights legislation, for extension of the right of education or protection of the rights of minorities, have, when clearly spoken, not been without public effect. "Would you want to be in a world where everyone does it?" is in a sense a reformulation of the Golden Rule onto the social scale.

Its most logical implication is to remind us to ask critically what the world would be like if every nation felt called to police half of it, or what a society would come to be like if everyone were a soldier. Especially the pacifist implications become clear if one recognizes the illogic of limiting generalizability to one nation. If everyone in this country were a conscientious objector, then by the same hypothetical miraculous conversion it would not be unrealistic to posit that at least most people in most other countries would also be considerably more peaceable than they are today, and would constitute much less a threat.

After all, it is the traditionally pro-military argument which uses this appeal most readily. "What if everybody did it" is, next to "what if a burglar . . . ," the argument which seems to be the most self-evidently convincing to those who have not thought much about this question. Making the "people" or the "ruler" the proper agent of ethical decision is one of the most un-challengeable axioms of the non-pacifist mind.

XI.
The Pacifism of Absolute Conscience

"I cannot serve as a soldier," said Maximilianus, "I cannot do evil; I am a Christian." Dion told him: "In the retinue of our lords . . . there are Christian soldiers and they serve." Maximilianus replied, "They are responsible for their own doings." Maximilianus was sentenced to death and the sentence was immediately carried out.
— The story of a noble martyr, 295

It is undeniably a part of human personality, or at least of the personality of certain men, that they are possessed by an undeniable, irrefutable, immediate conviction of right and wrong. This "conscience" will be nourished and given content by experience and education, but in the immediacy of its claims upon the person, and in its choice of when to be exercised and how deeply to be concerned about certain issues, it cannot be fully explained by educational considerations. It expresses itself by using all kinds of arguments, and may in the course of time in turn be modified by all kinds of arguments, but at the moment of immediate certainty, its claim for obedience is not debatable nor can it be tested by any criterion outside itself. The immediate conviction of conscience short-circuits the logical linkage between general moral considerations and particular conclusions.

It is *axiomatic* in current American usage that a man's conscience will tell him "yes" or "no" in ways he can *neither doubt nor explain.* It is this immediate and immeasurable absolute of "conscience" which government respects in its recognition of "conscientious objection." As recent U.S.A. experience demonstrates, governments would rather not have the conscientious objector be too articulate about his position or too able to make selective application to different kinds of situations. Indeed, if it is not an immediate and irrational position, it does not qualify for some people's understanding as "conscience." If an objector's position is too rational and selective, it is rejected as not "conscientious" but "philosophical."

Thus it is that most of the traditional ethical systems teach that it is the duty of an individual to obey the dictates of his conscience even if he should be wrongly informed. The integrity of the person is the presupposition of all morality; then in the short run and in the presence of inadequate information, it is better to preserve that integrity by obeying conscience than to do the objectively right thing while thinking it wrong.

This position has serious shortcomings. It is

subject to no theological or moral criteria outside itself. The autonomous conscience is therefore just as likely to be idolatrous as obedient. It escapes every kind of moral accountability and community. It is quite possible to be utterly sincere and utterly wrong; it is also possible to be doing the right and somehow not feel right about it.

Nevertheless, in a society (such as the Christian church) where not everyone can or should be a professional ethicist constantly able to re-inspect every link on the chain between general principles and concrete choices, that "shortcut" represented by "conscience" is indispensable. There must be certainties not constantly re-examined, if we are to go on with the work. Their claim on a man's allegiance must be more than rational, else he would spend all his energies negotiating about their fringes and loopholes. Whether "conscience" be in some inexplicable sense the voice of God, or a distillate of the social memory of the individual, such a logical short-circuit, which honors and fosters the individual's moral integrity by giving him a clear way to practice saying an unambiguous, "I cannot do otherwise," is far more wholesome both socially and psychologically than either a hardened, unquestioning conscience or an artificially maintained permanent anguished openness.

After all, the alternative seems to be an equally irrational and irresponsible blind acceptance of the behavior patterns or the legal demands of the surrounding society. To do "conscientiously" whatever one is told by the state to do is morally just as unaccountable as promising to obey the inexplicable dictates of one's own insight.

90

XII.

The Pacifism of Redemptive Personalism

*"Governments rather depend upon men
than men upon governments. Let men
be good, and government cannot be bad.
If it be ill, they will cure it. But if men
be bad, let the government be ever so
good, they will endeavor to warp and
spoil it to their tune."*
— William Penn, 1684

Man is at the root of all evil. Therefore man
is what must change if the evil of the world is
to be changed. Man cannot be changed by reliance
on the same kind of evil which already is the
mark of his misery. Violence perpetuates evil
by continuing the chain of evil causes and effects,
condemning men to the vicious circle of continuing
hate and destruction. No amount of greater
power or of greater modesty in using evil against

evil will get at the root of the problem.

The "personalism" of which we speak here is "redemptive," i.e., it makes a new start *at its own expense*. The redemptive personalist will refuse to cooperate in evil, will break the chain of evil causes and effects, and will take upon *himself* the suffering which this brings upon him, as an expression of his respect for the person of the adversary. Nonviolence in this form is an appeal to the conscience of the person with whom one deals. The readiness to suffer arises out of the recognition of the dimensions of evil and the impossibility of conquering it without suffering its evil effects. This position can very fittingly be taken by Christians but it may meaningfully be taken by others as well.[32] Its most substantial and theologically rooted Christian form is the Quaker understanding of "That of God in every Man."[33]

Without denying the reality of institutional structures and responsibility, this personalism discerns at the center of most institutions a man or a team or a clique, capable of turning the helm for the worse by their selfishness or for good by their renewed insight. The willingness to suffer at the hands of those responsible persons is a testimony of respect for them, and sometimes the only way to communicate to them an awareness of their responsibility for what they are letting be done to those whom they oppress — or of what they do to themselves by being oppressors.

It is *axiomatic* for the personalist that the problems of historical structures cannot be solved on the level of historical structures. This is not where the evil lies. We therefore accept (as everyone else must do in his own framework as well) that it is not possible to solve all problems. Redemptive personalism will not agree that its rightness or wrongness is to be measured by whether it can solve them all. No other position can do that either. All problems could be solved, however, if men would let their hearts be touched. Reaching those hearts is therefore the only significant task even if there are many cases where it cannot be done.

This position has serious shortcomings as a social strategy. Its willingness to accept working only "from below" is at best slow and sometimes defeatist. The trust which it places in the possibility of winning persons is easily mistaken for an ungrounded trust in the inherent redeemability of man. If this trust be thought to be rooted in fact, the position will be undermined at the first experiences of radical evil. The position therefore can be held only by those for whom it is deeply rooted in some ground of faith beyond experience.

This position is in danger of being philosophically subservient to a particular view of human personality; it may give up too easily on the structures of society, or it may hope too easily in the possibility of their being completely turned around by the conversion of the person bearing responsibility at the top.

Nevertheless, there is no alternative to personalism. What cannot be done by persons will not be done. Overarching structures and institutions may amplify or dampen, twist or straighten what men do, but still men will do it. This position is both more realistic and more promising than one which assumes that persons are of no significance and that the movement of history is a machine in which institutional forces impersonally push one another around. The word for that assumption is despair, even if it calls itself "realism." The humanization of personal experience demands that we run the risk of trusting personality even where this risk is objectively not justified. The only alternative is to run our society even farther into the ground by gambling on the assumption that impersonal forces are the most valid and the most powerful.

After all, while *recourse to war* is often justified by appeal to nonpersonalistic categories, especially to nonpersonal ways of conceiving of the enemy, in the *waging of war* there is a great element of personalism, even personality cult reflected in the larger-than-life stature given to key military personages by journalism and then by memoirs. Historians of war and diplomacy are fond of digging out the moment when the outcome of a particular battle, or even the whole course of a war was settled by one man's momentary emotional state.[34] There is in the military enterprise also a strong personalistic concern to "win the hearts of the people." Sometimes it is "firmness" and sometimes it is "benevolence" in the "pacification" process which it is thought will win the respect and the trust of an occupied population.

XIII.
The Pacifism of Cultic Law

"The Noncombatants. While recognizing that warfare is unavoidable in maintaining civil government in a world of sin, noncombatants conscientiously object to taking human life. They do not, however, condemn those who take part in war. On the other hand, noncombatants are willing to aid their government in every consistent way in time of warfare, except by taking human life . . ." [35]

The term "cultic" refers, according to one stream of current usage, to a position taken on grounds that seek no reasonable explanation, where neither results nor causes, general principles nor motivations are calculated. A "cultic" position is taken simply on the grounds that it must be taken, that the demand for it has been divinely revealed as such, without linking the judgment into a larger system of meanings and values. This kind of pacifism may, for instance, seek to be totally obedient to the biblical prohibition of the shedding of blood, whether this be thought of as specifically stated in the sixth commandment or otherwise. The obligation is absolute, but it is also arbitrary. One can, like the Seventh Day Adventists, refuse to kill and yet be willing to participate in the military enterprise, since it is only the act of doing the killing oneself which is forbidden.

The *axiom* underlying this position is that if we properly interpret revelation as the basis of obedience, there is no room for calculating or interpreting. There is not even any reason to try to discern underlying principles (as in variety III above) and to obey them consistently. Ours is only the task of keeping the rules clearly. For those matters to which the revelation has not spoken, we do no necessary service to God by trying to extend them gradually or to make deductions from them.

There are serious disadvantages to this position, which come to the surface even more clearly than in the somewhat similar case of "revealed principles." The process of internal testing which enables one genuinely to appropriate an ethical position, making it one's own so that one can confidently live within it, is undermined if we are to ask for no explanations and applications, if ethical obligation is arbitrary. Nor is it clear what kind of message one has to the outside world of those who have not chosen to listen to our peculiar source of specific instructions.

Nevertheless, like the positions of absolute

revelation and absolute conscience, this immature vision of the nature of ethical obligation may constitute a valid shortcut in the life of communities and of persons who have not the luxury and leisure of working through all the intellectual dimensions of a decision. If moral guides are to be accepted in implicit faith, then let us rejoice if they are rules which foster reverence for life.

After all, the only alternative to a cultic moralism which reverences life seems to be the equally cultic, arbitrary, unaccountable, and ungeneralizable obligations of patriotism, which is probably the only alternative for persons who make decisions on this level. The way the guerrilla efforts of Che Guevara in Bolivia, or of the several Palestinian Arab groups, are evaluated morally by their supporters has about it this same kind of unconcern for efficacy, accountability, morality. The imperative of the battle is self-sustaining; its transcendental rootage is subject to no critique. If the cultic rule which I impose upon myself is an abstention from killing, it at least does not actively and institutionally go about sacrificing others to any irrational commitment, as does most warfare.

XIV.
The Pacifism of Cultural Isolation

*"Our family has always been Menno-
nite. We have never taken part in war.
That is because we have nothing to do
with the world and its ways. It has
nothing to do with us what the world
does. It would go contrary to our fore-
fathers to go to war."*
— *Old Colony Mennonite*

It is quite possible for a segregated social group
to feel so much at home in its own subciviliza-
tion and so alienated from the larger society that
the concerns and values of the larger society have
no attraction or obligation. There is thus no
self-evident duty to defend what the larger society
is defending, to be in favor of its political order
or willing to fight for its freedom.

Every ethnic group has its own particular
language and cooking and style of life; it just
happens to be the cultural peculiarity of some

Mennonites[36] that they have in many different times and places avoided military service. Toward this end they migrated out of the countries which introduced universal military training — from Prussian lands in the 1780s, from Russia and from Alsace in the 1870s. Like the plain coat or *Plattdeutsch*, this practice has come to be sacred through the many generations of its association with the Mennonite culture. Yet it is not the only possible position for Christians to take and one would in fact hesitate to expect Mennonite behavior of an "Englishman," i.e., anyone not part of the subgroup. One would certainly not want to suggest that a non-Mennonite who does not share the nonresistant position is any less Christian. It would in fact seem incongruous if any significant numbers of persons without Mennonite upbringing were to find the Mennonite ethos convincing.

The *axiom* underlying this position is an acceptance of one's own identity, family, and culture as a divine gift. To be a person is to be local, parochial, and provincial; this local identity is to be received with thanks as a gift from God, and to be cherished, not *despite* the fact that it is strange but precisely *because* it is a rare and curious heritage.

There are serious ethical disadvantages to this position. It recognizes no missionary responsibility to the world around; it gives up on any possible wider acceptance of its own position. The same reasons which keep its own members faithful within the separate culture will normally be expected to operate so as to keep those "outside" just as faithful within their nationalistic, militaristic frame of life.

A further practical weakness of this position is the crumbling of the cultural barriers of the isolated community. It becomes increasingly difficult to maintain enough contact with the developed world to have a market for one's agricultural goods and a source of the necessary minimum of manufactured goods, without becoming open to cultural accommodation as well.

Nevertheless, everyone to be human must to *some* degree accept his born particularity and his limitations; for any "wider world" to which one might prefer to "escape" is equally particular and provincial, just on a larger scale. There is no Christian community, and there is no wider humanity, which is not thus provincial. The Amish and Hutterian subcultures just might be the most viable autarchic communities left in the West outside the mainstream melting pot.

After all, a provincialism which eschews violence and renounces any imposition of its own standards on others — even of its Christian standards on other Christians — is to be preferred to the violent provincialism of war which is ready to destroy others to defend its own apartness. No one has more irrevocably given up on the world outside his in-group than he who is willing to destroy a portion of it.

XV.

The Pacifism of Consistent Nonconformity

"Because not for us is the wrestling against blood and flesh." Nothing could be plainer than that it is a general principle for life that earthly combat and struggle is never the portion of the Christian disciple. One could as well argue that the command for the children to obey their parents only applies on Sunday, as to claim that spiritual warfare applies only to spiritual activities.

— *James R. Graham*, Strangers and Pilgrims

The "dualist Mennonites"[37] and the Hutterian Brethren are not merely isolated. Their apartness may also be taken as the most appropriate Protestant example of a rejection of military force which is derived from a still more sweeping and still more basic rejection of the world in all its forms. "The military" is not simply an instrument for killing if necessary; it is the quintessence of most other sins as well; of theft and deceit and adultery, of pride and pomp and power hunger.[38] The demand for military service is the point at which the surrounding world most pressingly intervenes into the life of the separate community and most systematically and vigorously seeks to change its character and its lifestyle. It is thus at this point self-evident that the person committed to a life of nonconformity to the world must see the demand for separation focused in its starkest form.

This rootage of rejection of participation in the military within a deeper sweeping nonconformity liberates the Old Order Amish Mennonite or the Hutterite completely from any obligation to explain how he would run the world without force, how he would solve the problems which violence does not solve, how he would defend his family, etc. He has chosen the better part. It is not for him to dictate or even to suggest how those whose spiritual loyalty is to the values of this world could achieve their own ends without using their own means. He may follow the logic of his social dualism so far as to say that what is wrong for him might be right for them; or he may simply suspend judgment. In either case the worldings' problems and needs, the distress and the defense of their society are none of his concern.

The *axiom* underlying this position is that "the world," in the radically rebellious sense of that term which is characteristic of the usage of the New Testament's General Epistles and John's Gospel, is a reality; not simply a state of mind but an empirical network of institutions and ways of behaving. This "world" has as its definition its rebellion against the will of God and its self-glorification. Being an empirical reality, it can be seen and must be shunned. Any witness to it, any missionary presence in its midst, must be subordinated to the duty first of all: to have identified it and taken a stance over against it.

This is a position with some very evident ethical disadvantages. It is, however, not proper to condemn it as hastily as many do as being expressive of a consistent rejection of the world or opposition between "Christ and culture."[39] This is the most illogical misinterpretation. Precisely because it discerns worldliness as a cultural reality, and identifies those worldly cultural practices which are to be avoided, this position more than any other is committed to creating a Christian cultural alternative to the world. This is immediately evident in any survey of the ways in which ever since the sixteenth century, Hutterian and Amish separate communities have been culturally creative. They have succeeded beyond any other comparable populations in creating and maintaining a nearly self-sufficient civilization with its own mores, characterized by love for the land and efficient use of it, craftsmanship, strongly supportive social relations, nonviolent sanctions upon deviance, and its own solutions to the problems of survival and identity. Over against the depersonalizing effects of mass education they have created not a culture vacuum but an alternative pattern of cultural transmission and value definition which, as we said before, just might be the only subculture capable of surviving in North America outside the mainstream. Whatever is wrong with the Amish and Hutterian patterns, it is not that they are against culture.

The real disadvantage is rather a fruit of their cultural strength. The power of this community to recreate itself in its progeny brings it about that within a few generations there are within the church numerous members who are committed only superficially or grudgingly to its values. There is thus "world" inside the church. With growing awareness of other Christian groups, one cannot avoid recognizing as well that there is also church outside "in the world." But such a recognition must seriously undermine the group's confidence in its own mission.

Yet the deeper flaw is the way in which such a systematic rejection of the wider world becomes a hidden dependence upon it. Whatever the outside society does, we must do otherwise. Thereby the church is dependent upon the world which she rejects but which she still permits to dictate the patterns of her rejection.

Nevertheless it is the case that war is eminently representative of the structured insurrection of mankind against the loving will of God. There is such a thing as a fallen *kosmos* which the Christian should not love, and the *sword* is characteristic of it. Killing is the first sin in Genesis 4 and the primary example of sin in 1 John 3. Jesus was tempted by violence as He was not by sloth, gluttony, lust and the other standard sins. It is the only sin which is always irrevocable; other sins
104

may destroy the one sinned against, while killing always does.

After all, the same type of monolithic thinking about the world tends to prevail on the "other side" as well. Those Christians who accept war in principle because of a decision of principle to accept the world and because acceptance of the world on its own terms is in all circumstances the best thing to do (the so-called "hard Niebuhrians") tend to be the least capable of discriminating moral judgment within that involvement.[40] Thus a categorical decision to accept the wrong in the world on its own terms, taking war as the eminent example of this acceptance, is even less morally free, and even less realistic about the power of sin, than is systematic nonconformity.

XVI.

The Non-Pacifist Nonresistance of the Mennonite "Second Wind"

"*The term nonresistance as commonly used today describes the faith and life of those who accept the Scriptures as the revealed will of God, and who cannot have any part in warfare because they believe the Bible forbids it, and who renounce all coercion, even nonviolent coercion. Pacifism, on the other hand, is a term which covers many types of opposition to war. Some modern pacifists are opposed to all wars, and some are not. Some who oppose all wars find their authority in the will of God, while others find it largely in human reason.*"

— *Guy F. Hershberger*, War, Peace, and Nonresistance

In a survey of the logically possible options we have not generally sought to be representative of denominational experience. We have not labeled some positions as "Catholic" and some as "Quaker," though we could have. Seldom is a particular denomination, at least for very long, representative of only one line of interpretation. There is, however, one contemporary exception to this generalization, namely a particular movement in recent North American Mennonite experience in which a quite specific new understanding has been brought about by the encounter with other currents of thought. The problem which surfaces here is worthy of observation beyond the limits of the denomination. The reason for including this type of pacifism here is not the presumption that the reading audience has suddenly become Mennonite. Nor is it a sudden attempt by the author to speak for or against a part of his own tradition. Rather, in keeping with the purpose of the book as a whole, its reason for inclusion is that it is known as an ideal type far beyond the bounds of its own confession.

Already on the surface of language usage the problem is visible: the word "pacifism" itself became a subject of controversy. This can be illustrated simply by comparing the texts written by leading denominational thinkers in the past generation.

John R. Mumaw, then a Bible teacher and later president at Eastern Mennonite College, wrote in the midst of World War II a pamphlet, "Nonresistance and Pacifism"[41] in which the argument was strongly presented that the posi-

107

tion taken by Mennonites with regard to war, traditionally labeled as "nonresistance," has very little in common with the modern Protestant phenomenon known as "pacifism," especially in the form which it had taken between the two World Wars.

Beside it we may place the article, "The Pacifism of the Sixteenth-Century Anabaptists," read to the American Society of Church History in December 1954 by the denomination's then most prominent historian, Harold S. Bender.[42]

These two qualified Mennonite spokesmen were describing what they would both have testified was basically the same position. One of them accepted as a description of this position the label "pacifism," to which he then gave a specific description out of Mennonite history. The other began by assuming that the same word already had a contemporary meaning, given to it by the usage of others, which designated a position he rejected; rather than trying to "redeem" the word by giving it his own proper meaning, he preferred to reject it.

It is probably due to the cultural image of Mennonitism in the public mind that the usage favored by Professor Mumaw was most widely perceived beyond the denomination. John C. Bennett considers Mennonitism as paradigmatic for what he calls a "strategy of withdrawal"[43]; Thomas Sanders takes the same line with the characterization "apolitical."[44] Mennonites are a "pure type"; they represent one possible position with great integrity.

Something similar happened, for other reasons,

within the denomination as well. This matter of vocabulary brought to the surface a long-simmering problem of cultural and theological identity. As American Mennonites first began to seek to communicate to the English-speaking world around them, just before, during, and after World War I, the temptation was natural to identify naively with any kind of available "peace position" over against all kinds of militarism and nationalism. In this connection there was a certain sympathy for the anti-war movements of the period between the first two World Wars; to this we owe the acceptance of the phrases "historic peace churches" and "peace witness."

But then there came a serious second look. Most Mennonites were powerfully impressed by the differences which separated them from the pacifisms of the Peace Pledge Union and the Fellowship of Reconciliation. Some of the positions taken by those "pacifists" were not specifically Christian in their orientation. Some of them placed so much trust in the goodness of men that they had not faced the deep need for suffering in the cause of divine love. Some of them were not ready to pay the price for full consistency in the rejection of all war. Some of them were unjustifiably optimistic about the capacity of an unregenerate society to solve its problems without breakage.

They seemed to promise a changed motivation, suggesting that war could be abolished by *fiat*. They failed to recognize the moral compromise in their own willingness to resort to nonviolent types of coercion, or to make exceptions for a "peace-keeping" army; if it were international.

In their optimism about doing away with violence within a society they failed to observe that the threat of force is part of what keeps the peace.

In the rebound from this discovery of clear differences, some Mennonites then reversed their orientation and came to conclude that except within a nonresistant separated church there is no foundation at all for nonresistance; so that in some sense at least war is "right for the government although it is wrong for us."[45] This kind of thinking was favored by the desire to be somehow intellectually acceptable. It was suggested by thinkers like Reinhold Niebuhr, who were willing to recognize Mennonites as being right in their place, as having understood Jesus well, if in return they would grant that war is somehow right for governments. Or in other cases, the "mainstream" position to which one conformed was that of a more traditional Protestant orthodoxy, which taught a separately revealed set of moral obligations for government different from those binding upon the individual Christian.

This temptation to dualism was favored in addition by the cultural accommodation through which American Mennonites had gone in the last few generations. If one limits nonresistance to oneself, one can then be nonresistant and still patriotic and anti-communist; one can be accepted within denominational pluralism and within patriotic small-town society without representing a challenge. One can live up to one's own rules, respect the dictates of one's own conscience for oneself. This is an especially attractive temptation for those who had already partly slipped into the understandings of the meaning of their resistance which we have described as "cultic" or "cultural" or "separated" (XIII-XV).

Another thrust in the same direction was Mennonite involvement in the fundamentalist controversies of this same epoch. Critical modern theologies could write off the holy wars of the Old Testament as due to the primitive culture of the time and therefore not relevant today. Mennonites could not so easily forget Joshua and David and Josiah. It was simpler to set the Old Testament/New Testament tension parallel to the world/church tension. Capital punishment and war are proper for the Jews, and the world, but not for New Testament Christians.[46]

There thus arose a systematic dualism, in which the position which Mennonites preferred (following the older German usages, "defenseless," and Matthew 5:39) to call "nonresistance" was carefully distinguished from pacifism in general and from nonviolent activism in particular. Mennonites since 1940 have thus invested as much concern in keeping their distance from "pacifism" as they have in denouncing militarism; in fact the military have their place in the non-Christian world, and some Mennonites commend the violence of the state, as long as they need not be a part of it.

The unspoken *axiom* underlying this position would seem to be double; socially, it assumes that if you are complimented on your integrity, you should accept the compliment. The Niebuhrian analysis, while rejecting the "sectarian" position as proud and irresponsible, concedes to it both consistency and that it under-

111

stands Jesus aright. Rather than look twice to test the sincerity or the hidden assumptions of such a backhanded compliment, dualistic Mennonites, gratified for a place in the sun even if it be under a shadow, accepted the challenge and set out trying to be consistently "apolitical."

Intellectually, this view assumes that a clear division of labor between two realms or "worlds" or "levels" is a step forward in understanding. Once this is done you need only ask of each moral issue in which area it lies, and the problem is solved.

This position has several kinds of shortcomings. One type arises from the fact of its recent origins in efforts to fasten upon Mennonitism a structure of interpretation borrowed from its critics, rather than one growing out of its own experience; the analysis does not fit. It hides from Mennonites the broad (conservative) political meaning of their participation in the national economy, in educational and professional life. It hides as well the (critical) political impact of their freedom to emigrate, their conscientious objection, their service agencies. It leads them to seek to deny their very real sympathies for specific political options and for outspokenly religious statesmen. They cannot really feel comfortable in applying to active churchmen in high places (Dulles, Hatfield, McGovern) an analysis whose original axiom was that the state is pagan.

But the weakness of this view is not only that it does not fit the life of the group it seeks to represent. It is equally questionable on other grounds as well. It implicitly denies both missionary and ecumenical concern, since in effect "Christ

112

is Lord for us but not for them." It accepts as if it were a compliment the judgment of political irrelevance pronounced not only on "sectarians" but also thereby on Jesus by mainstream theologians. It concedes to government — though somehow seldom to communist governments — a mandate to wage war which goes far beyond the substance of the New Testament view of the State.[47] Often it mixes this with the theocratic imagery of the Old Testament holy wars, as if every modern government were somehow an equivalent of ancient Israel. It hastily denies the inherent close relations which Mennonites could well have to other peace movements, on the grounds of criticisms (humanistic optimism, irrealism about sin and power) which would apply even more to the military alternatives. Any known militarism after all shares all the vices of non-Christian pacifism. Militarism as well as pacifism is humanistic and utopian; it places enormous trust in the wisdom of administrative bureaucracy, in the moral insight of persons who have been hardened to think of other men as worthy of extermination. To entrust peace and freedom to the military establishment, to trust a person with powerful weapons to be morally self-critical, places greater and more unjustified confidence in human character than does any kind of pacifism. Every kind of trust in weapons is just as non-Christian in its moral assumptions and certainly more unchristian in its activities than the comparable types of humanistically overconfident pacifism.

Nevertheless, this view may well claim the pastoral and pedagogical merits of the "cultic"

113

and "isolation" views (XIII-XV) whose dangers it shares as well. Its radical oversimplification makes it possible for a religious community to survive and to understand itself in lay language. If it were the case really (or should we say "when and where it is the case concretely"?) that immediate political relevance and faithfulness to Jesus' word and example are alternatives, then the disciple of Jesus will of course choose faithfulness at the cost of withdrawal. Such a placement of the alternatives is itself not according to the gospel, nor is the assumed definition of "relevance" underlying it; this is where "apolitical" Mennonite has been misled. But once the question is thus posed (by the ecumenical interlocutor) the "sectarian" answer is the better one of the two options he has been given.

After all, every possible way of justifying war also introduces a similar radical dualism, according to which what is wrong elsewhere is right in war. The theological mainstream agrees that one cannot follow Jesus, in the way the sources say He said He wanted to be followed, and face the politician's problems. As naive, unmissionary, and potentially self-righteous as this neo-Mennonite dualism is, it is still less so than the alternative it rejects.

XVII.
And On and On . . .

The list above may seem long enough, and perhaps it is if our goal was to dramatize the multiplicity of logics that may move men to renounce war. Yet it should not be thought that the list is complete. There are noteworthy persons, traditions, movements which would not yet find themselves fairly represented by any one or any combination of the above statements. Without an analysis as long as those proffered above, we may still recognize the presence of these remaining gaps by means of a few briefer characterizations.

A. There is the pacifism of *the eschatological parenthesis*. It is represented today by Jehovah's Witnesses and by some dispensationalist Protestants, and was held to in the sixteenth century by Melchior Hofmann and perhaps by Hans Hut. It has some basis in the apocalyptic literature of the biblical age.

There is a change coming soon in world history, it affirms, which divides that history into two portions. The present dispensation is one in which the will of God for His people is faithfulness in

115

suffering. But after the imminent inbreak of the new regime, God will destroy His enemies; and He may well make use of His faithful people in that judgment. The rejection of warfare in the present is then not the application of a generally nonviolent set of ethical principles. To be guided by such principles without regard to time would be to deny the sovereign governing freedom of God as He prescribes for each age a pattern of faithfulness which is not calculating but simply obedient. It is not ours to reason why, but it is ours *in this age* to be ready to die. No kind of calculation or justification of behavior in terms of motive or effectiveness is relevant; God has prescribed the where and the when of our suffering now and of our triumph soon. Those who share now in His long-suffering with rebellious man will one day share in the triumph of Armageddon.

Incidentally, it is possible for this "parenthetical" logic to work the other way around just as well. Logically, this should not surprise us, since the shifting of regimes from one age to the next is not according to human reason, but dictated by divine sovereignty. The Scofield Annotated Bible, probably the most widely read current medium for this view, reserves the ethic of the Sermon on the Mount to a future "Kingdom age," since for it to have become binding, the Jews would have had to accept Jesus as King.

B. There is the kind of pacifism generally referred to as "anarchic," represented in recent years by some youth within Students for a Democratic Society. Here the sense of the meaning of social movement is such that the most needed

116

social contribution is to obstruct the functioning of the existing evil establishment. It is not felt that it is the responsibility of the protester to assure the availability of a better alternative structure or solution, or even to guarantee that his own interference will be productive. The only criterion is that of radical disavowal of the present. It is assumed that if the present system is forced to "grind to a halt," then anything else that can come next would be certainly better. The rhetoric may speak of "taking over" but this does not involve the implementation of a clear alternative strategy already available and waiting to be put into effect by the seizure of power. This position is a "pacifism" in that the military establishment is very near the center of what it disavows; it is, however, not a complete position, but rather an unstable or impermanent mixture of utopianism (VIII), nonviolent direct action (V), and just war (II).

C. There may be such a thing as a consistent Asian *pacifism of self-negation.* If all outward human history is either illusion or inexorable impersonal necessity, if my living is hopeless, or if my goal is blessed release from life and from desire, if the acceptance of suffering for its own sake or as spiritual discipline is one of the highest goals, if contradiction can never be disentangled into clean yes and no options, then what is worth fighting for? The ends which are called on to justify war fade away in the concrete social and political despair in which Asian man lives or in the misty light of the religions whose call to man is that by accepting hopelessness he can find release from deceptive desire. Now there is a clear element of caricature in this description. It is a capsule statement of how "the East" is sometimes perceived by an un-understanding "West." Nonetheless even in caricatured form this perspective remains significant as a critique of the compulsiveness with which Western man is convinced he must bring about righteous ends, soon, by his own power.

D. There is the pacifism *of the very long view.* All of the discussions about what must be averted by war point to an evil which is likely to take place in the near future. Yet we should have learned by now that short-range appearances often deceive and that the long-range movement of history is often determined by factors quite different from those which dominate the consciousness of those who think they are making crucial decisions.

All political reality is so morally ambiguous that however sure we are about the relatively greater justice of a given cause, the difference cannot be so much as to justify the absolute recourse such as war represents. We know so little about how things will turn out that any impatient preoccupation with insuring the right short-range results may be condemned not because it breaks some moral law but because it is shortsighted and impatient.

There is a kind of pacifist argument which says that the aggressor and the defender are morally not very different because both are using violence; this Reinhold Niebuhr answered long ago: "There is a perspective from which there is not much difference between my egotism and that of a gangster. But from another perspective there

118

is an important difference." [48] But in the sober long view suggested here the point is that the opposition in war is not between the gangster and myself, or between policeman and criminal, but between two policemen or between two gangsters, and that with the special danger — to which Reinhold Niebuhr elsewhere has pointed with special clarity — that a self-righteous policeman may well be worse than a gangster.

The loss of sovereignty might just be the way to survive. The Czechs in 1968 or the Danes in 1940, the inhabitants of the Gaza strip in 1968, or the Dominican Republic under the American invasion of 1966, could not choose the option of heroic resistance in any other form than that of surrender. In these cases the loss of national sovereignty may actually be the occasion for a renewal and revitalization of national identity, which often thrives under foreign occupation. Even more is it possible that the suffering or subjection of a people may be an occasion for growth and renewal in the Christian church.

A close relative of this *long-view* pacifism is the *modesty* concern; power is arrogant and corrupts its bearer; the claim to set the world right undercuts itself. This can be said theologically in terms of idolatry; or in sober political science in terms of arrogance. It is not a mere spiritual, pastoral counsel: "too much power goes to your head." It is rather a political mechanism; he who claims to impose righteous order on the rest of the world is himself a tyrant.

E. There may be a distinct coherent "pacifism of redemptive suffering." The willing acceptance of suffering is a part of the Gandhian method [49]

119

and of the Anabaptist and Mennonite "non-resistant" traditions,[50] yet for them the suffering is conceived as *instrumental*. It is the price of nonviolent resistance or a way to touch the heart. For others, the suffering itself may be seen as bringing about a healing or purgative effect in society, or in the mystical order of things.

At least about the distant past we are often able to say that tragedy had its fruitfulness. This is a possible generalization about suffering in history; it is a necessary Christian affirmation about certain kinds of suffering.

F. There is the ancient ethical tradition of the imitation of Jesus. It makes the same moral claims as the pacifism of moral law (III above) but its content is not abstract commands but the life and word of Jesus. His command and example are to be followed without calculation of social possibilities. Its major spokesmen have been Peter Waldo, Peter of Chelcice[51] and Leo Tolstoy. It does not expect widespread acceptance, but neither does it acquiesce in the world's noncompliance with Jesus' norm, as do the other minority approaches. (IX and XII-XV)

G. There is the pacifism of self-discipline. The center of moral obligation may be located in my responsibility to discipline myself. I may forbid myself to kill, or I may refuse to participate in the military machine, not because I cannot bring myself to hate and to kill, but because I can bring myself to do it too easily; because my propensity to hatred and to violence makes me aware that it is at this point that I need, if I am to be human, to govern and tame the very forces which the military life unleashes and glorifies. In this connection, then, the logic does not center upon the action itself but upon my responsibility for the kind of person I make myself by what I do. This differs from the "virtuous minority" approach by its individualism, from the "utopian" by its concrete self-discipline, from the "personalist" by its being more concerned for the evil in one's self than for the adversary. It is compatible with the "moral absolute" and "absolute conscience" approaches, but more flexible in its psychological awareness.

H. There is a "situational pacifism." Two or three fads ago, Americans were reading paperbacks on ethics by Joseph Fletcher, James Pike, and others, advocating what they (incorrectly) called a "new morality." Underlining the need for moral decision to take into account the specific situation, exemplifying the decision process with abundant anecdotal illustrations of times when it seemed that one would "simply have to" do something that was "against the rules," they argued that the decision-in-the-situation is a distinct, and a correct, mode of ethical reasoning. As ethical approaches go, this one turned out to be most unhelpful, for every case of "simply have to" turns out on analysis logical to be just another "rule," albeit an unavowed one. To explain why one "must" do what seemed to be forbidden by one rule, one points to another ethical generalization about values which, it is held, is in this situation of greater weight.

Nonetheless, the currency of contextualist rhetoric does loosen up ethical discourse so that some are willing to take positions on visceral or intuitional grounds, or on unconscious casuistic grounds (like II above), which they are unable to explain or feel no need to articulate responsibly. They reject a given war, at a given time, for themselves, without sensing any duty to test the validity of their arguments by measuring other wars or challenging the decisions of other people.

XVIII.
The Pacifism of the Messianic Community

*"The hint half guessed, the gift
half understood, is Incarnation."*
T. S. Eliot.
*"It is not by accident that the writer
of 1 Peter said that Jesus carried men's
sins 'in his own body.' Because it
happened in Jesus' body, it can also
happen in ours."*
— *Walter Klaassen*, What Have You to
Do with Peace?

The more carefully and respectfully one has
sought to interpret the positions of others, the
more difficult it becomes in presenting one's own
view not to make it benefit unfairly from com-
parisons. Probably the critical observer would
discern in this last position as well a combination of several distinct strands, which might

be further dissected.[52]

To say that this is the pacifism of the *messianic* community is to affirm its dependence upon the confession that Jesus is Christ and that Jesus Christ is Lord. To say that Jesus is the Messiah is to say that in Him are fulfilled the expectations of God's people regarding the man in whom God's will would perfectly be done. It is therefore in the person and work of Jesus, in His teachings and His passion, that this kind of pacifism finds its rootage, and in His resurrection that it finds its enablement.

When we confess Jesus as Messiah we find His uniqueness and His authority not alone in religious teachings or in spiritual depth but in the way He went about representing a new moral option in Palestine, at the cost of His death.

It follows that the character of such a position can be known only in relation to Jesus Christ. This simple sentence is a statement first of all about the nature of revelation. Just what it means to believe in Jesus as Christ, just what it means to follow Jesus Christ as revealer of the nature and will of God, cannot possibly be figured out on our own resources. This position is thus comparable to the "absolute principle" and the "cultic" positions described before (III, XIII) in that it makes its appeal clearly to something that man must be *told*. Yet it varies from them decisively in that the *telling* has come to us not on a tablet of stone chiseled by the finger of God alone on Sinai, or from the mouth of a prophet, but in the full humanity of a unique and yet complete human being. It might be pointed out that whereas all of the positions reviewed above are

124

held by Christians, this is the only position for which the *person* of Jesus is indispensable. It is the only one of these positions which would lose its substance if Jesus were not Christ and its foundation if Jesus Christ were not Lord.

Since Jesus is known in His full humanity as a man responding to needs and temptations of a social character, the problems of our obedience to Him are not problems in the interpretation of texts. Nor is the question of our fidelity to Him one of moralism, a stuffy preoccupation with never making a mistake. The question put to us as we follow Jesus is not whether we have successfully refrained from breaking any rules, but whether we have been participants in that human experience, that peculiar way of living for God in the world, of being used as instruments of the living of God in the world, which the Bible calls *agape* or *cross*.[53]

When we speak of the pacifism of the messianic *community*, we move the focus of ethical concern from the individual asking himself about right and wrong in his concern for his own integrity, to the human community experiencing in its life a foretaste of God's kingdom. The pacifistic experience is communal in that it is not a life alone for heroic personalities but for a society. It is communal in that it is lived by a brotherhood of men and women who instruct one another, forgive one another, bear one another's burdens, reinforce one another's witness.

We did not make that point as we went down the line of varieties, but it could have been pointed out along the way that the major streams of pacifist experience (except for the particularly
125

withdrawn communal ones (IX, XIV, and XV) tend to be represented by powerful individuals, persons perhaps with numerous sympathizers but few followers, no congregation, and only limited success in creating a movement.

Let it not be thought that this community resource is merely a moral crutch or a psychological springboard which enables individuals to feel more free and confident as they take pacifist positions. The social meaning of a peace witness is far more fundamental than that. The existence of a human community dedicated in common to a new and publicly scandalous enemy-loving way of life is itself a new social datum. A heroic individual can crystallize a widespread awareness of need or widespread admiration: only a continuing community dedicated to a deviant value system can change the world.

This position has serious disadvantages when measured by the standards of the critical ethicist. It is not for all men. Those who uphold it would affirm that the discipleship of which they speak is a necessary reflection of the true meaning of Jesus and that the call to follow Jesus is a call addressed to all men. But the standards by which such a life is guided are not cut to the measure of men in general. They can be clearly perceived — to say nothing of being even modestly and partially lived — only through that reorientation of the personality which Jesus and His first followers called repentance. Repentance initiates that true human existence to which all men are called. But as long as a given man or a given society has not undergone that change of direction, it is not meaningful to describe how he or they would live

126

as pacifists. It is thus not possible to extrapolate from this stance of faith a strategy for resolving the urban crisis tomorrow. It is not a position which can be institutionalized to work just as well among those who do not quite understand it or are not sure how much they believe in it.

It is for many a further disadvantage that this position is utterly dependent upon who Jesus was and the attitude one takes toward Him. All positions mentioned above call for some kind of commitment and some kind of faith, all of them are minority positions which can be taken only by someone willing to run risks and be different. But, as we said, only this position collapses if Jesus be not Christ or if Jesus Christ be not Lord. For some kinds of Christians this is, and for others it is not, a disadvantage; for most habits of ethical deliberation it is a serious one. Even Christian theologians generally dedicated to making Jesus normative in their thought about deity and the creeds, tend to be startled by the suggestion that He might be indispensable in defining a proper political humanity.

Another disadvantage of this position is that it does not promise to work. The resurrection is not the end product of a mechanism which runs through its paces wherever there is a crucifixion. There is about the Christian hope in the kingdom that peculiar kind of assurance which is called faith, but not the preponderant probability of success which is called for by the just war theory or by a prudential ethic.

Nevertheless, this position is closer than the others to the idiom of the Bible and to the core affirmations of the Christian faith. It reckons

127

seriously with the hopelessness of the world as it stands and yet affirms a gospel of hope. It shares the integrity of the "absolutist" views (III, VIII, IX, XIV) without their withdrawal from history, and the practical concern of the programmatic views (II, IV, V) without placing its hope there.

After all, the invocation of violence to support any cause is implicitly a messianism; any national sense of mission claims implicitly to be a "saving community." You cannot avoid either messianism or the claim to chosen peoplehood by setting Jesus or His methods aside; you only cast the aura of election around lesser causes.

XIX.

What Have We Learned?

Careful meditation upon this variety of patterns of thought may throw some light on our conversation about Christian faithfulness today.

A. It is easy to distort the discussion about the Christian and war by transmuting it into a comparison of ethical systems. The critical reader will have noticed as we moved through the inventory above that in most cases the kinds of models of ethical thought with which we were dealing represented attitudes not simply to war but to the whole problem of ethics. Arguments of almost the same form could have been presented section by section for dealing with marital fidelity, truth telling, or art. The post-Niebuhrian non-pacifist will see all pacifism, as he rejects it, as utopian purism (VIII or IX) or as withdrawal (IX or XIII-XVI), rather than recognize a respectable pacifist argument when presented in his own term (II or IV). The "situation ethics" advocate will reject pacifism for its inflexible principles (III, VIII) rather than take seriously those pacifisms which calculate carefully in the situation (II) or which preserve the integrity of the loving disposition of free decision in every context (XI). One is then not discussing war but talking past one another out of logically incompatible prior assumptions. Each kind of pacifist position has its rootage in a wider context and should fairly be evaluated only there.

B. The argument around pacifism is only one of the points where the multiplicity of our models of ethical thought becomes manifest. Academic Protestant ethical thought in the past generation has been largely dominated by the social-responsibility models of the Brothers Niebuhr, while academic Catholic thought has been comparably dominated by older principle-application models. Might the manifold diversity of the approaches displayed above (quite apart from their pacifist proclivities in the cases chosen) not call us to a less monochromatic practice of ethical theologizing? Each of these logics (as we noted under the rubric "nevertheless") has its own integrity; which in each case we were able to criticize but not really to refute. Must we seek to boil each one down to where we can call it an inferior version of some other approach?

C. From our plea that each type of pacifist reasoning be respected in its own right, it should not be inferred that a position which holds "purely" to one of these types will be more worthy of respect, or more effective, than one which blends them. While certain mixtures may make for serious moral or practical confusion, especially when pragmatic arguments (IV) or "just-war" reasoning (II) are interlocked with some of the others, it may well be said that a position which weaves together more than one compatible strand will be more convincing, more effective, and more viable. The positions of Martin Luther King, Jr. (IV, V, XII, and perhaps III), of the *Catholic Worker* (I, III, VI, IX), and of Anabaptism (III, IX, XIV and XV) are such fabrics where the several threads reinforce one another.

D. A final "in-group" word might be addressed to the attitude of those dualistic Mennonites (XVI) who, by eschewing pacifism, risk an unavowed and uncritical nationalism. Their point is well taken; there are many kinds of pacifism held to by many kinds of Christians for many kinds of reasons (to say nothing of several more non-Christian types which we have only hinted at here), and they should not be confused. Yet, having recognized this, it is time for nonresistant Mennonites to move beyond their initial defensive reflex to the recognition of a real degree of practical common conviction which they do and properly should share with non-Christian pacifists or (much more) with non-Mennonite Christian pacifists. This is not a total agreement, but at every point it nevertheless represents a greater degree of commonality and a clearer recognition of common adversaries than when Mennonites are so concerned to stand clear of pacifism that they become unconsciously but practically covert militarists.

There is certainly a real sense in which Christians in any country, and therefore also Mennonite Christians in the United States, are not simply "Americans" like all their neighbors.

131

Nevertheless it would be more nearly correct, and contribute more logically to reasonable discussion, to say that they are Americans of a particular kind, i.e., Mennonite Christian Americans, than if they were to deny their origins and identity and pretend to be Russian or Argentine or Vietcong. Likewise it would contribute more to sober conversation if, instead of fixing upon an irrational avoidance of the word "pacifist," Mennonites would recognize with more precision and responsibility the varieties of ways in which men are led, sometimes by intelligent analysis and sometimes by emotional revulsion, sometimes by irrational optimism and sometimes perhaps by the Spirit of God, to recognize the wrongness of war and to devote themselves to the service of their fellowmen, even though in other ways or under other labels and with other understandings, than those a historic peace church has found most adequate. The Christological nonresistance of the Radical Reformation or the "Historic Peace Churches" is *nevertheless* one form of Christian pacifism, and most honest when it is ready to be counted as such.

E. It could be claimed, after analysis of the entire assortment, that any ethical system, if taken seriously, as more than self-justification, can, and that some ethical systems must, lead to one kind of pacifism or another. These various pacifisms are sometimes compatible with one another, sometimes even mutually reinforcing (XIII-XVI, or I, II, and IV), sometimes directly contradictory in their assumptions (IV versus VIII, IX, or XVI). Yet they are no more so than the varied reasons men have for participating in war. In their denunciation of war, however it be explained, the moral commonality of all of them is greater than the systematic diversity. There is no ethical system, no morally responsible stance a Christian can take, to which one form or another of the pacifist appeal cannot be addressed. There is no serious critique one can address to the pacifist which does not, if taken honestly, (as indicated above under the rubric "after all") turn back with greater force upon the advocate of war.

Notes

1. This is especially the case when spokesmen for the same position can sometimes accept and sometimes reject the same label. That this is the case in at least one tradition is demonstrated below, Chapter XVI.

2. It would be a fascinating exercise to cross-reference all the logical types here described with the texts gathered in the two best anthologies on the subject: editor Peter Mayer's *The Pacifist Conscience*, Henry Regnery Co., 1967, and the Weinbergs' *Instead of Violence*, Beacon Press, 1965. We shall not attempt this. The degree of complexity and coverage already attained is sufficient to make the point of this essay. We shall note parallels to the major strands lifted up in G. Nuttall's *Christian Pacifism in History*, Blackwell, 1958.

3. A papal message of December 1967 said, "The word peace does not mean pacifism, it does not hide a cowardly and lazy conception of life. . . ." This slurring apposition is more understandable in view of the word's usage in the European languages, for which "appeasement" is probably a better translation than the literal equivalent "pacifism." It is not focused upon the practice of conscientious objection. It refers to the projection, not necessarily for idealistic reasons, of a nonmilitant policy for a nation.

4. A sample of the limitation of this approach is evident in the reproaches which have since been cast on the memory of Pius XII for failing, as some judge it, adequately to risk his pastoral status by roundly and publicly condemning the Nazi genocide.

5. At the same time that Benedict XV was pleading for peace (some of his statements are gathered in Harry W. Flannery, ed., *Pattern for Peace*, Newman Press, 1962, pp. 9 ff.), a propaganda pamphlet, *La Guerre Allemande et le Catholicisme*, was published under the editorial direction of the rector of

the *Institut Catholique* of Paris with a preface by the Cardinal Archbishop of Paris. Within a few months the response of German Catholics was printed: *Der deutsche Krieg und der Katholizmus; Deutsche Abwehr franzoesische Angriffe*, with a German cardinal's telegram as frontispiece. To note this religious provincialism is not to suggest that Protestant provincialism is morally any less reprehensible; but at least it does not give the lie to the claim to be one visible ecclesiastical communion.

6. The best general introduction to "just war" thought is *War and Moral Discourse* by Ralph Potter, John Knox Press, 1969.

7. *The Divine Imperative* (ET 1936) here quoted from the 1947 edition, Westminster, pp. 469-74.

8. A now familiar case in point is the misunderstanding of Karl Barth's near pacifist position. See J. H. Yoder, *Karl Barth and the Problem of War*, Abingdon Press, 1970, pp. 73, 103-5.

9. The term "selective objector," which accentuates what distinguishes him from other conscientious objectors rather than what stands at the center of his own position, came into current use first in the late 1960s. The logic and respectability of its claims were given formal recognition in 1968 by the World Council of Churches and by Catholic and Lutheran bodies in the U.S.A. Cf. James Finn, *A Conflict of Loyalties: The Case for Selective Objection*, Pegasus, 1969.

10. The only serious efforts to make the just war theory relevant by looking concretely at current military options and *not* saying no at some point (counter-population, nuclear threats, chemical and bacterial warfare, CIA coups against constitutional governments, clear-and-destroy tactics against entire populations in rural Vietnam) jettison their own credibility by making it inconceivable how they could ever say no in some other conceivably still worse case.

James Douglass, in a chapter headed "Anatomy of a Just War," *The Non-Violent Cross*, Macmillan, 1968, pp. 155 ff., attempts to challenge Paul Ramsey to admit that the classic just war criteria if honestly used must condemn all modern war, and its preparation as well. Ramsey responds in his "Can a Pacifist Tell a Just War?" *The Just War*, Scribners, 1968, pp. 259 ff., that if Douglass were consistent he would not bother with the question. This exchange is disconcerting not only in its timing (with Ramsey responding to Douglass' argument before it was published) but also in its substance. Douglass intertwines respect for the objectivity of just-war theory with doubts about its honesty and with ambivalence about its concern to moderate a relative justice in a fallen world, in such a way that it remains unclear whether he thinks the doctrine a help or a hindrance. Ramsey in return undermines his own claim for the objectivity of the just-war tradition by his *ad hominem* claim that a pacifist cannot read it straight, and dodges completely the quite legitimate question whether an effective no to a particular war on the basis of objective policy criteria is really still possible for Ramsey, as it was in 1961 (*War and the Christian Conscience*, Duke University Press, pp. 151 f.) and still in 1965 (*Again, the Justice of Deterrence, op. cit.*, p. 357). By discussing with great finesse the changes he has or has not made in his thought about the concept of deterrence or about the advisability of legal provision for selective objectors, Ramsey turns our gaze away from the absence of equal attention to the refinement and the institutional expression of the same criteria as they might be applied in the negative case.

11. A lively sample of this kind of movement is the article, "A Reluctant Pacifist," contributed by Andrew J. Good, Jr., to *Concern*, United Methodist Board of Social Concerns, Washington, for January 1, 1968. Trying to be honest with Jesus and to safeguard the possibility of ever saying no has here driven an honest man with no prior sectarian orientation to the conclusion that he must begin by saying no now.

12. This reference to the function of a principled statement in the structure of ethical thought is not linked to the linguistic interpretation of a particular statement such as that of the Decalogue. The prohibition of "murder" does not, in Exodus 20:13 or Deuteronomy 5:17, literally exclude all taking of life, either on the etymological level or in the wider context of the Mosaic codes. But as Jean Lasserre has demonstrated (*War and the Gospel*, Herald Press, 1962, pp. 165 ff., esp. 170 f.), the capacity of the church to draw general moral guidance from the Decalogue has at no other point been limited by a legal-literal-minimal interpretation of its meaning. Covetousness, false witness, adultery, or idolatry could also be given a minimal ancient-Hebrew meaning in catechesis, but they are not. Let it then not be thought that the theological-ethical claim to be made for the sanctity of life is dependent upon a linguistically naive appeal to the Mosaic words.

13. Johannes Ude, *Du Sollst Nicht Toeten*, Hugo Mayer Verlag, Dornbirn (Austria) 1948.

14. The ecumenical statesman J. H. Oldham, responding to the German bombing of Coventry, spoke categorically against the bombing of civilian populations, while freely conceding that the threshold between unjustifiable and justifiable weapons of

war is not unambiguous: "I agree that the line is hard to draw; I am sure that there is a line to be drawn somewhere. Christianity has no meaning unless for every man there is a point where he says: 'Here I stand before an absolute: this is unconditionally forbidden,'" *Christian News Letter*, No. 48, 25 September, 1940. However many ways there are to challenge it theoretically, the axiom "there must be a line somewhere" seems still to be structurally indispensable to moral communication. This indispensability is not wiped away by saying that the line could be drawn somewhere else, or could bend; the question remains, "Do you ever draw any line?"

15. The classic statement of this critique is Niebuhr's "Why the Christian Church Is Not Pacifist," in *Christianity and Power Politics*, Scribners, New York, 1940. Cf. as well Franklin H. Littell, "The Inadequacy of Modern Pacifism," *Christianity and Society*, Spring, 1946, pp. 18 ff.

16. In the midst of the Paris peace talks of February 1969, U.S.A. negotiator Henry Cabot Lodge was quoted as warning his counterparts that "violence is no solution." He was addressing himself to the Hanoi/NLF claim that there could be no peace without a new regime in Saigon. Even amidst a struggle in which both parties have assumed for decades that violence is a justifiable way to a solution, namely the organized violence of guerrilla and counter-guerrilla war, it still seemed self-evident and not at all ludicrous to Mr. Lodge that a *coup d'-etat* or change of regime in Saigon would be wrong because it would "seek to solve a political problem with violence."

17. The most serious examples of how this may be done, though on a very modest scale, are the study papers which Quakers have addressed to the problems of disarmament, China, and Vietnam. With informed seriousness they encounter real political options, quite without moralistic short-circuiting of structural problems.

18. In addition to the literature of the Gandhi and King movements, with their extensive attention to techniques and training, there have been numerous serious studies in The Netherlands (*Nieuwe Weerbarheid*, Arnhem, 1952, *Geweldloze Weerbarheid*, Amsterdam, 1965) and in the Anglo-Saxon world (cf. the bibliography of Peter Mayer *op. cit.*, especially the sections pp. 442 f. and 451 f.). Those who assume as self-evident that violence is the only useful tool have generally not studied this literature. A sample of recently multiplying German literature is the work of Theodor Ebert: *Ziviler Widerstand*: Fallstudien . . . (Bertelsmann, 1971). *Civilian Defence:* Gewaltloser Widerstand als Fom der Verteidigungspolitik (Bertelsmann, 1970). *Gewaltloser Aufstand*, Freiburg, Verlag Rom-

bach, 1969.

19. Some of the objections to a "programmatic" approach are those cited above. Another is a form of the objection to "principled ethics" to which we referred in Chapter II. Somehow he who rejects pacifism as unfree (Karl Barth, for instance) sees in the refusal of war a moral bondage which he does not equally perceive in its acceptance. To be "programmatic" may be a vice in pastoral counseling, but there is no alternative in politics.

20. "As a matter of fact, it is the non-pacifist, not the pacifist, who believes that after a long-drawn-out orgy in indiscriminate killing and wholesale destruction people may be expected to think rationally and act justly. The pacifist has no such confidence in human nature." Ernest Fremont Tittle in Weinberg, *op. cit.*, p. 153.

21. "Aren't you bothered by the equally trivial truth that human affairs — surely precisely because they are in God's hand — on both the small and the large scale — tend with a certain regularity to take some completely different course than had been foreseen . . . because the most important realities of the future, when it has come present, usually rise up so surprisingly that the previously prepared calculation must be crossed out?" Karl Barth, "Letter to an American Churchman," October 1942, in *Eine Schweizer Stimme*, Evangelischer Verlag, p. 289.

22. Nonviolence understood as an effective tool, of course belongs within the family of the "programmatic" approaches (IV); we nonetheless describe it separately because of the uniqueness of its picture of "peace," its creativity as to method, and its fusing of personal and structural interior and foreign political concerns.

23. Richard Shaull offered a "reflection" on "The Political Significance of Parabolic Action" at a ceremony where draft cards were turned in, in the context of the University Christian Movement's "Week of Process '67," *Motive*, April 1968, p. 27 f. Shaull indicates awareness that such an approach involves certain kinds of risk, but does not suggest what they are, what damage they might do, or how to determine whether they are worth taking.

24. Hans-Werner Bartsch, "Das Soziale Aspekt der urchristlichen Paranese . . . ," *Communio Viatorum*, Vol. V, 1962, p. 255.

25. The most pointed portrayals of this approach are in the exegetical works of Hans-Werner Bartsch and Dietrich Fischinger: cf. Bartsch's article, "A New Theological Approach to Christian Ethics" in John C. Bennett (ed.), *Christian Social Ethics*

in a Changing World, Association, 1966, pp. 54 ff.

26. The reader may note that the Spock-Coffin *et al* case in 1968 changed its character in midstream. It began as an outspoken act of civil disobedience, aiding and abetting refusal to observe the draft, because the laws on that point were deemed unjust; but then it was transmuted into a test case with the claim that the highest law of the land was on the defendants' side.

"The exigencies of a conventional defense against the conspiracy charge often seemed on a direct collision course with the needs of the anti-war movement." Jessica Mitford, *The Trial of Dr. Spock*, Alfred A. Kropf, 1969, p. 173.

27. This use of casuistics is exemplified by my article, " 'What would you do if . . .?' An Exercise in Situation Ethics," in the *Journal of Religious Ethics*, Vol. 2, No. 2 (1974), 81 ff.

28. Among the studies on utopian societies is Harry W. Laidler, *History of Socialism*, Crowell, 1969 (revised).

29. Mark 8:35 and parallels: "Whoever would save his life will lose it, and whoever loses his life for my sake and the gospel's will save it."

30. Especially is this the case for the views which express the duality geographically or culturally (below XIV-XVI). There is less danger of this when the minority lives amidst the society whose mores it judges, as in the models of St. Francis or the *Catholic Worker* houses.

31. A capsule vision of the message of this movement is offered by Cornell and Forest in *A Penny a Copy*, The Macmillan Company, 1968.

32. Gandhi, King, and Lanzo del Vasto would fit in here; though other strands of their emphasis would also belong under types V, VI, and IX. In the Gandhian movement this concern for winning over the adversary is very closely linked with a concern for the discipline of one's self. The fasts which Gandhi imposed upon himself, were not conceived as threats to make the oppressor feel guilty of his suffering or possible death, but rather as self-purgation because Gandhi and his followers had failed in self-discipline. This dimension of personalism is dealt with separately below in Chapter XII.

33. Cf. especially G. Nuttall, *op. cit.*, pp. 50 ff. "The Dignity of Man."

34. Cf. the article "The Wrong Rubicon: LBJ and the War," by Tom Wicker in *Atlantic Monthly*, May 1968, according to which the bombing of North Vietnam was decided upon in one particular conversation between President Johnson and Ambassador Lodge three or four days after President Kennedy's assassination. This article is part of a larger work on "The

Influence of Personality on Politics"; a further demonstration that personalism is not a peculiar weakness of pacifists.

35. *Instruction and Information Manual*, "Seventh Day Adventists and Civil Government," National Service Organization . . . , Washington, pp. 11, 12.

36. Mennonites, especially their Old Order and Old Colony branches and their Hutterian cousins, are probably the most visible and typical example of this kind of pacifism. Yet there are parallels in other traditions (Old Order German Baptist Brethren, Molokans). Many other ethnic-religious groups would take an analogous attitude toward other doctrinal or ethical issues than that of pacifism.

37. "Consistent Nonconformity" should not be identified with one branch nor with all, as it is a tendency within most branches but not normative in any but the Old Order groups.

38. ". . . killing in war . . . calls in question, not merely for individuals but for millions of men, the whole morality, or better, obedience to the command of God in all its dimensions. Does not war demand that almost everything that God has forbidden be done on a broad front? To kill effectively and in connection therewith, must not those who wage war steal, rob, commit arson, lie, deceive, slander, and unfortunately to a large extent fornicate, not to speak of the almost inevitable repression of all the finer and weightier forms of obedience?" Karl Barth, *Church Dogmatics*, Vol. III/4, Edinburgh, 1961, p. 454.

39. The simplest and most widely read case of this misinterpretation is in H. Richard Niebuhr's *Christ and Culture*, Harper, 1951, p. 56, with specific reference (his only reference) to Mennonites.

40. Cf. the *Christian Century* editorial "The Power, Not the Glory," May 1958.

41. Mennonite Publishing House, Scottdale, Pa., 1944, reprinted 1952.

42. Reprinted in *Church History*, June 1955, and in *Mennonite Quarterly Review*, January 1956.

43. The basic source cited by non-Mennonite analysis of Mennonite positions is not the Mumaw pamphlet but rather the chapter "Nonresistance and Pacifism" in G. F. Hershberger's *War, Peace, and Nonresistance* (Herald Press, 1944 and 1953). John C. Bennett, *Christian Ethics and Social Policy*, Scribners, 1946, pp. 41 ff., Culbert Rutenber, *The Dagger and the Cross*, Fellowship, 1958, pp. 17 ff., and Thomas Sanders, *Protestant Concepts of Church and State*, Holt, 1964, pp. 102-4, report on the intra-Mennonite discussion.

44. Sanders, *op. cit.*, pp. 75 ff. How widespread this understanding is can be seen in the fact that H. R. Niebuhr (note 32 above) can take it for granted, without needing to document or explain.

45. "The basic function of the political order is to maintain order among sinners through the use of coercion. . . . This order is ultimately maintained through police, jails, court, G-men, militia, and armies. All are contrary to strict New Testament standards, though the Bible sets aside all anarchism by sanctioning government for those who do not live on New Testament standards. This is the example, par excellence, of the necessary evil!" Donovan Smucker, "A Mennonite Critique of the Pacifist Movement," *Mennonite Quarterly Review*, XX (1946), pp. 81 ff.

46. This interpretation can appeal to one major strand in sixteenth-century Anabaptist thought, most simply stated in Art. IV of the "Brotherly Understanding" of Schleitheim (February 1527): "The Sword is an ordering of God outside the perfection of Christ. It punishes and kills the wicked, and guards and protects the good. In the Law the Sword is established over the wicked for punishment and death, and the secular rulers are established to wield the same." Here "Law" means the Old Testament; "secular rulers" means sixteenth-century civil governments.

47. Cf. our text on the meaning of *Romans* 13, in my study on the political significance of Jesus, soon to be published by Eerdmans.

48. *Christianity and Power Politics*, p. 169.

49. Gandhi's strategy fits none of our molds; it blended fruitfully elements of Nos. IV, V, and XII as well.

50. It is the acceptance of suffering which Geoffrey Nuttall considers to be most typical of this view: *op. cit.*, pp. 32 ff.

51. Cf. Nuttall's chapter, "The Law of Christ," *op. cit.*, pp. 15 ff.

52. From the author's own position only those strands are gathered here which are most relevant to this essay's concern for distinguishing among diverse styles of thought.

53. Cf. note 50.

Index

John H. Yoder has been professor of theology
since 1965 in the Associated Mennonite Biblical
Seminaries of Elkhart, Indiana. He has also taught
in the universities of Notre Dame (Indiana) and of
Strasbourg (France) and in the *Instituto Superior
Evangelico* of Buenos Aires, Argentina.

Prior to 1965 he served in Europe and North
America with the relief and mission agencies of
the Mennonite churches.

Other publications (in addition to those listed on
page 4) have dealt with the areas of reformation
history, missionary methods, church renewal, and
the ecumenical movement.